MIMESIS INTERNATIONAL

PHILOSOPHY
n. 34

Ann Van Sevenant

THUS REPLIED ZARATHUSTRA

MIMESIS

© 2020 – MIMESIS INTERNATIONAL
www.mimesisinternational.com
e-mail: info@mimesisinternational.com

Isbn: 9788869772252
Book series: *Philosophy*, n. 34

© MIM Edizioni Srl
P.I. C.F. 02419370305

TABLE OF CONTENTS

NOTE TO THE READER — 11

FOREWORD
by Jenny Rose — 13

PREFACE — 15

INTRODUCTION: THUS REPLIED ZARATHUSTRA — 19
    Opening act — 19
    Primal scream — 21
    First awakening — 23
    Discerning mind — 24
    Nature's order — 26
    Eyes of the heart — 28
    Response-ability — 30

PART ONE: HOW? — 33
    Responding to injustices — 33
    False leaders — 34
    Resistance — 35
    Daring to reflect — 37
    Two tendencies — 39
    Tripartite motto — 40
    Primordial choice — 42
    Freedom of choice revised — 43
    Life and non-life — 45
    Happiness — 47
    Social practice — 49
    A friend and a foe — 50
    The invention of confidence — 52

PART TWO: WHO? ... 55
    Iranian prophet? ... 55
    Companions ... 56
    Glad tidings ... 59
    The light metaphor ... 61
    Confidential friendship ... 62
    Process of abstraction ... 64
    Cult of fire ... 67
    The plant metaphor ... 69
    Growth ... 71
    Proto-ecology ... 73
    Zoroastrianism ... 74
    Zoroastrian division ... 76
    Universal dimension? ... 78

PART THREE: WHAT? ... 83
    The birth of orientalism ... 83
    Interpreting the *Gathas* ... 85
    New terminology ... 87
    Good and evil? ... 89
    The twinning ... 91
    Two abodes ... 93
    Weigh bridge ... 95
    Final judgement? ... 97
    Self-regulation ... 100
    Cosmodicy ... 103
    Progression ... 105
    New times ... 107
    Regeneration ... 110
    Completeness ... 112
    From East to West? ... 114

PART FOUR: WHERE? ... 117
    Zoroastrian heritage? ... 117
    Middle East and Egypt ... 119
    Zoroastrianism and Judaism ... 121
    Greece ... 123
    Iran ... 126
    Persian philosophy ... 128

Neoplatonist renaissance and Sufism 131
Spain 132
Italian renaissance 134
England 136
France 139
Germany 141
India 144
Para-Zoroastrianism 146
The revival of the Silk Road 148

PART FIVE: WHEN? 151
Call for justice 151
Renewing the message 153
Ignored freedom 155
Nietzsche's Zarathustra 157
Eurasia 159
Remain true to the earth 161
Relapse into non-life? 164
Contemporary approach 166
Philosophical ecology 168
Ecosophy 171
Timeless reply 174
Indirect action 176
Arch-practice 178
Re: Zarathustra 181

In memory of Abtin Sassanfar
In memory of Kersee Kabraji

"Regenerated make my life and true"
(34,15)

NOTE TO THE READER

Thus thought Zarathustra is the title of an academic study that I published in French (*Ainsi pensait Zarathoustra. Une philosophie avant la lettre*, Paris, Non Lieu, 2017). With a wink to the book of Friedrich Nietzsche, *Thus Spoke Zarathustra*, I emphasised the gap between our thinking and our speaking, between our words and our actions. Already in the second millennium BC, the ancient Iranian thinker Zarathushtra Spitama was aware of this human condition. His proto-philosophical thoughts – known to us under the form of *Gathas*, hymns or songs – make of him an existential philosopher *avant la lettre*.

My special thanks to Michael Whitburn for proofreading the manuscript.

JENNY ROSE
FOREWORD

It takes both confidence and personal conviction for a scholar to seek to bridge the epistemological gap between knowledge derived from the secular, intellectual study of a particular religion or philosophy and the central metaphysical or 'spiritual' concepts of that faith tradition. Most academics who tackle the complex issues relating to the putative development of the Zoroastrian religion tend to focus either on its historical significance throughout the millennia from the earliest epigraphic attestation of 'Mazda worship' to its current expressions of belief and rituals, or on the interpretation of its texts from a linguistic or functional perspective. As a philosopher with a particular interest in poetics and aesthetics, who has published her research in several languages, and who for many years has undertaken a personal study of the words ascribed to the ancient Iranian thinker, Zarathustra, Ann Van Sevenant is uniquely placed to engage in a connective endeavor that encompasses differing forms of knowledge.

Dr. Van Sevenant's work considers the various approaches from within the context of her understanding of the 'infinite wisdom' expounded by Zarathustra in the *Gathas*, the Old Avestan 'songs' attributed to him. She pinpoints the primary momentum of these ancient texts as resonating through their attention to the 'discerning mind', identifying as 'protophilosophy,' the vision and dynamism that she perceives articulated in their 'proto-ecological' verses. In this work – which distills certain elements of her earlier *Ainsi pensait Zarathoustra: Une philosophie avant la lettre* – the author introduces the poetic 'chants' as presenting challenging ideas for any epoch, which might serve as catalysts for individual change, and also impact wider society and the natural world. The organic relationship between the microcosm and macrocosm remains as germane for the human condition now as ever, and this current work hones in on the relevance of the *Gathas'* dramatic presentation of the existential and social forces through the ages to the present, with the emphasis on personal choice between that which brings 'life' or 'non-life'.

Ann Van Sevenant does not claim here to offer a neutral, prescriptive account of the religion that owes its name to Zarathustra, but seeks – in an almost stream-of-consciousness manner – to address a series of questions concerning the applicability of this ancient yet 'universalisable' philosophy to the timeless challenges of being human.

Dr. Jenny Rose
Claremont Graduate University
November 2019

PREFACE

In most Western university studies, Greek philosophy is considered as the most ancient kind of wisdom. The oldest fragment of philosophical thinking is ascribed to Anaximander, one of the Ionian thinkers in Asia Minor (6th century BC). Mostly, the rise of ancient Greek philosophy is presented as a process of detachment from Greek mythology, the tales of the gods invented by mankind in order to explain nature. The first philosophers tried to explain nature by reason, by using rational concepts in contrast to the practices of veneration and doubtful sacrifices.

What was left out in that presentation is that the Greek philosophers did not invent philosophy all by themselves. We must remember that the Greeks conquered an empire with a long tradition and that they were profoundly influenced by it. It is not unimportant to consider that the Indian and Persian civilisations were at least more than a thousand years older. And that the Persian Empire conquered by the Greeks was based on ancient Indo-Iranian knowledge. The Greeks were fascinated by concepts like wisdom, truth, happiness, friendship.

Around 3000 BC, Indo-European nomads coming from the north split into two groups, the Vedic Aryans and the Iranian Aryans. The word arya means noble, worthy of respect, with no reference to biological characteristics. The Vedic Aryans settled in the valley of the Indus River, while the Iranian Aryans headed for the Iranian Plateau (Iran means literally the land of Aryans). What we know about these cultures has been carefully preserved in texts that can be consulted today, respectively the Vedas and the Gathas. They constitute the oldest collections of thoughts known to humanity.

The Vedas originated in the Indian subcontinent and are written in Vedic Sanskrit. They form a body of knowledge that was transmitted by Indian wise men into Vedism, Brahmanism and Hinduism. The oldest texts date back to around the fifteenth century BC. They were composed by ancient Aryan thinkers who transmitted their visions in the form of hymns and mantras. Today, not all Indian schools of philosophy base their reflections on the Vedic scriptures, but many of the used concepts can be traced back to this ancient wisdom.

The Gathas are less known. These hymns are as old as the earliest Veda and originated to the east of northeast of modern Iran. They are attributed to the ancient Iranian prophet Zarathushtra Spitama (hereafter Zarathustra or Zoroaster), who lived between 1700 and 1400 BC in Central Asia. Recent studies indeed situate the life of the Spitama clan in the Bactrian region, in East Iran (Afghanistan today), in the second millennium BC. Zarathustra's disciples, called the Magi – the root of the word magic – moved from the east of Iran to the west, to Babylonia and beyond. These Magi honoured the values of the Zoroastrian tradition, namely free choice, responsibility, honesty and respect. Plato admired the Persian values and Aristotle was influenced by this great culture, as is testified in a number of texts. Moreover, the Jews in exile experienced the reality of these values, when they were liberated in Babylon by the Persian king Cyrus in the sixth century BC.

The Zoroastrian way of life was a guideline both privately, for individuals who try to be honest, and publicly, for leaders who practice what they preach. It was based on the understanding that it is better for everyone to be trustworthy and just. This meant that the followers of this Persian wisdom were required to admit that words and deeds did not always correspond, and that they were prepared to admit the divide between thought, word and action. In accordance with the motto of Zarathustra "think well, speak well, act well", these three registers – thinking, speaking, acting – were constantly being taken into consideration. Awareness and self-examination do indeed demand regular exercise. Zarathustra considered self-deception and the deception of others to constantly be lying in wait.

While European scholars in the West were familiar with the Vedic hymns from the 18th century onwards – which inspired philosophers like Schopenhauer -, Zarathustra's hymns did not receive the same attention. They were mingled with later Avestan texts and were not identified as a separate section before 1858. Nietzsche had a partial knowledge of the Zoroastrian wisdom and way of life, although his thought was not free from a Manichean interpretation. In fact, Western thinking was based on the mind-body dualism and since Descartes, the debate was concentrated on the opposition of reason and heart, spirit and soul, intellect and passion. Philosophers like Kant and Hegel tried to find a way to reconcile these oppositions using a third element.

In the 19th century, the East began to be a source of inspiration for the West and from the 20th century onwards, it became a response to Western decadence. Eastern philosophy on the whole was based on the three elements of mind, body and soul. Whereas Indian thinking was more oriented towards worship and veneration, Chinese knowledge concentrated on the cooperation of mind and soul as a means of providing an equilibrium and an energetic vital force. Confucius and Lao Tze considered physical exercises as a way of empowering the correspondence of mind, body and soul. The Zoroastrian way of life, then, was more directed towards mental exercises and self-examination, based on the choice of fighting unjust behaviour. By engaging in an existential path towards consistency, the emphasis was on the exploration of one's potential.

In this book, we direct our attention to the thoughts ascribed to the ancient Iranian thinker Zarathustra. The reader may find they are insufficiently known, even in the Zoroastrian religion. As will become clear, they were a source of inspiration in Mesopotamia, Egypt, Greece and Asia Minor, and were revived in Persian philosophy and poetry. Either they were altered by thinkers like Mani, who adopted them to favour his personal religion in the third century AD, or they played an imported role in the Italian Renaissance. When the first translation in French appeared, they were invoked by freethinkers like Voltaire in his quest against the power of the church and individual thinkers like Hume, Kant, Hegel or Nietzsche, who became familiar with this original view on life and felt inspired by it.

What I find most unpalatable in the 'post-truth era' is that we seem to ignore the existence of a 'pre-truth' philosophy; of a proto-philosophy that emphasises not 'the' truth, but trueness. Never before have we been confronted with such a variety of falseness, of hiding behind appearances. This is clearly related to the many possibilities that exist in our societies of faking our conduct, of getting away with abuse, crime and sheer fraud. With new technologies allowing improper use, we seem to succumb more easily to questionable practices. And so, the inclination to mislead and to hide becomes less offensive. And what is more, the increasing power of falsehood leads us to neglect the existence of our inherent potential to fight hypocrisy and deception. This potential is present in every human being, but when indifference begins to gain ground, we feel deceived by others and become inclined to copy them.

The question thus arises whether it is at all possible to address the silent killer within. Zarathustra's dream was to awaken people and gradually make them aware of the other kind of existence they could lead. The most fundamental element was to ignite the flame of happiness and keep alive the fire to resist mental imprisonment. With his thought-provoking reflections, Zarathustra tried to explain to his companions that self-respect can be regenerated, as well as respect for each other. He made them aware of their capacity to reflect by themselves, rather than to turn their status, descent or ethnicity into a prerogative or a pretext for demanding privileges. If this message has been able to cross the borders of religions and cultures, of countries and centuries, it is because humanity time and time again depends on a renewed enlightenment. Caring individuals simply know deep down that nothing good will come from harming one another.

This introduction to what can be referred to as a proto-philosophy, is based on what is conveyed in the *Gathas*, these most ancient verses that encompass a revitalising wisdom. Zarathustra's reply to the many questions about life is that the capacity humans have to renew their viewpoints should not be discredited and that life energy should not be taken for granted. This makes all the more sense in the post-human era, when the planet is becoming increasingly populated by inhabitants who are prepared to destroy the life and beauty of plants and animals; when false leaders claim they will colonise outer space. There must come a time when false pretences are stopped. We are moving beyond the point of saving the idea that the planet can save itself, now there is no longer any doubt that humans are able to destroy the earth's regenerative capacity. The planet needs humans who urgently engage in a durable project and develop an ecological philosophy that can be put into practice by individuals who agree that besides human rights, we need human responsibility.

INTRODUCTION: THUS REPLIED ZARATHUSTRA

Opening act

A very ancient wisdom of which we have a record is attributed to Zarathushtra Spitama[1], who was looking for answers to the distress inside himself. The *Gathas* or 'songs' transmitted through the ages are divided in five metrical sections, with a total of 17 'chapters', starting with chapter 28 of the Zoroastrian liturgy, the *Yasna*[2]. In the first verses, we find an opening act with an interesting setting. Four characters are summoning each other. The characters are respectively the soul of mother earth (*geush urvan*), self-regulation (*asha*), good thinking (*vohu manah*), infinite wisdom (*ahura mazda*). The scene is presented like a theatrical drama with four actors, more precisely four epithets or representatives of Ahura Mazda[3].

Mother earth[4] is complaining: "Why did you create me? Who made me this way?". She rebels against the destructive power of humans: "I am

---

1 Opinions diverge with regard to the meaning of Zarathushtra, deriving from *zaratha* (golden) and from *ush* (to shine). 'Golden light', 'bright shining light' or 'brilliant star' are appropriate meanings that also relate to the classical Greek version of the name, the Greeks recognising *astro* or star. 'Zarathushtra' is the correct option, but in the West 'Zarathustra' is more frequently used.
2 The *Yasna*, the old Iranian title, is composed of 72 sections, among which the first five *Gathas* are numbered from 28 to 34 (on the choice of existence) and from 43 to 53 (on wise and good influence). Originally, the *Yasna* was a ritual that contributed to the reordering of the cosmos after periods of chaos.
3 There are six representatives, personified attributes of Ahura Mazda, forming the holy number seven. They rank first among the 33 *yazatas*, who are worthy of worship, later called 'angels'. In the plot of the first Gatha, only four out of six are implied, as kind of archangels. In later Avestan texts they are known as the 'holy immortals' (*amesha spenta*).
4 The 'soul of the cow' is a correct translation of *geush urvan* and is preferable to the 'soul of mother earth', though with a less literal meaning. It is a unifying

oppressed by anger, cruelty and aggression" (29,1). This primal scream is answered by infinite wisdom, the creator[5] of mother earth, who in turn puts questions to cosmic self-regulation: "Who can be her saviour? How may we bring comfort to her soul, offering protection (...) against the followers of deceit?" (29,2). The self-regulating principle answers: "Not one is known to me who protects the right-minded against the cheaters" (29,3). Together with mother earth, they turn to infinite wisdom with this one request, whether true persons can survive amidst the followers of deceit? (29,5).

Finally, infinite wisdom speaks to all three: "Was it not for this that all who receive the sweetness of mother earth, will serve and be her protectors and guardians?" (29,6), and turns to good thinking: "Who, according to you, shall help mankind?" (29,7). The answer follows: "I know of only one person who has listened to our teachings, Zarathustra Spitama. He is willing to proclaim through songs your infinite wisdom. That he be granted the power of speech" (29,8). As a result, Zarathustra is chosen by the four characters to lead humanity towards truthfulness.

Yasna 30 is about Zarathustra, who immediately takes on the mission he has been assigned. He unfolds his multiple questions, his world view, his call regarding tomorrows world, with this introductory line: "Now unto eager listeners will I speak" (30,1). In this light, he addresses the four characters both directly and indirectly, alternating with his audience, the eager listeners. The idea is that the attentive listeners not only hear what Zarathustra conveys, but that they also come in touch with their inner voice, "which is the greatest of all voices" (33,5). On several occasions, a most subtle connection between the inner voice and the four characters is suggested. Humans who are inspired by the representatives of wisdom may

---

element and symbolizes the primeval creature. In fact, there is a possible reference to Egyptian mythology and the cult of Isis, a goddess cow and guardian of the sun, which later becomes a goddess of plenitude and nourishment. She quenches the thirst of humanity with a divine liquid.

5   In most translations, the notion of 'creator' is used to refer to Ahura Mazda who is the originator of creation. Some translators also use the terms 'builder', 'organiser' or 'architect'. I refer to Antonio Panaino, The List of Names of Ahura Mazda (Yasht I) and Vayu (Yasht XV), (2002), cited in Almut Hintze, 'Monotheism the Zoroastrian Way', *Journal of the Royal Asiatic Society*, Volume 24, Issue 02 (April 2014, p. 228).

"grow strong and overcome deceit and misleading" (31,4). It is an essential guideline in Zarathustra's thinking.

Primal scream

In the preceding verses of Yasna 28, Zarathustra explicitly expresses his admiration for the four characters and he hopes his deeds are in accordance with respectively infinite wisdom, self-regulation, good thinking. With hands outstretched, he wishes to "bring solace to the soul of mother earth" (28,1)[6]. Also, the companions of Zarathustra are already present in Yasna 28 and they express the same concern and questions. The order of the *Gathas* is indeed not linear and on different occasions several voices are implied. This allows us to read these replies at three levels. Firstly, they are replies by Zarathustra to infinite wisdom that reflect his awakening. Secondly, they are replies offered to an external audience. Thirdly, they express the worries and the wishes of his followers.

After the reading of Yasna 28 and 29, we understand that the *Gathas* are structured as replies to the four characters, that the companions of Zarathustra are addressed and that the latter, once enlightened, become his followers. Let us now further examine the fact that Zarathustra heard the scream of mother earth; that he responded to the four characters who were in search of a person who would bring comfort to mother earth and protect her against deceivers. One cannot but notice that it is the character 'good thinking' who knows of one person who is willing[7]. In the present text, I intend to highlight this ability of good thinking. But before that, let us

---

6 Yasna 29 is somewhat interruptive. In the traditional order of the verses, preference is given to Zarathustra who in Yasna 28 expresses his songs of praise, as if he had already been appointed as the new leader. This might have been the reason why I.J.S Taraporewalla changed the order in his *Devine Songs of Zarathushtra*, but again followed the traditional order in *The Religion of Zarathushtra* (Bombay: India House, 1979).
7 The epithet *vohu manah*, has been translated as 'good mind', 'good thought' or 'good thinking'. I agree with the renowned translator Stanley Insler that the evolving aspect of the process of thinking should be underlined. Insler was devoted to the study of the syntax of the *Gathas*, which upset their translatability and made them accessible in a more comprehensible language. This reading has given rise to freer translations that are not always recognised by the academic community.

notice that Zarathustra's responsibility was ignited by the four characters who decided to give him the power of speech.

Indeed, Zarathustra is illuminated or enlightened; he wakes up from his sleep, his awareness or his consciousness having been awakened. This awareness – or potential awareness – was already present in a kind of responsibility preceding any engagement. As a matter of fact, Zarathustra responded before any call from the outside. He manifested a readiness to listen and to engage in good thinking, which is being confirmed by one of the characters, probably because his situation was no longer tenable. What actually happened to Zarathustra was the result of a kind of correspondence between the inner impression that something was wrong and the call to act responsibly, to activate the faculty to respond.

The structure of the initial play is neither that of the revelation of a secret knowledge, nor is it that of the appearance or manifestation of a deity. The initial scream reveals the need for change, and in Zarathustra the wish to learn how. In his appeal to be guided by wisdom, he wants to become a good guide, inspired by acts of love in the hope of overcoming the hatred of foes. This will therefore require the opening up of his mind and heart and the assistance of good thinking, so that the divine sparks can ignite. Or is it the other way round, that human responsibility is lit by a situation or by an instance that summons the person in question, with the latter recognising the ignition and trying to act accordingly?

Without trying to determine which was first – the primal scream or Zarathustra's readiness to listen – the fact remains that a whole series of questions follow. Throughout the *Gathas* many doubts and numerous questions are scattered. Most striking are the questions regarding the universe, the position of man on earth, the personal commitment. For instance, the verses in Yasna 44 all start with a question: "This do I ask". The question is repeated nineteen times. These verses are addressed one by one to infinite wisdom, to Ahura Mazda. They are uttered in an atmosphere of confidence and respect, Zarathustra awaiting a reply so that he may rightly comprehend. They concern the goal of life, the existence of nature's order, the striving for light, the protection from false leaders. They clearly express a need for assistance, a cry for help, an almost desperate call for relief.

First awakening

Almost fifty percent of the *Gathas* is formulated as questions. The other half is formulated in the form of responses. This formal aspect is not to be underestimated. The two series of questions in Yasna 44 are followed by a third series concerning the creation of the cosmos and the place of man in the cosmos. These questions are all marked by either a thirst for knowledge or impatient despair. In Yasna 48, Zarathustra asks: "When shall my friends arrive to spread the message?" (48,10); "When will dedication and trueness come, and rewarding service, bringing peace and rest? (48,11). In Yasna 51, the emphasis is on 'when?', Zarathustra awaiting a change in the current situation: "Who shall be friend to Spitama? Who shall come to Zarathustra's aid? (...) Who shall truly live within our brotherhood?" (51,11).

Initially, the questioning causes him to despair, with his powerlessness taking over from time to time. Zarathustra tries to reply to the call of responsibility. His increased awareness engenders turmoil, distress, existential struggle. Indeed, he is not simply floating ideas, at random. As he tries to overcome his doubts and solitude, to cope with his anxieties, to look for answers to questions about life, he addresses the "father of good thinking", that is infinite wisdom (31,8). Amid so much injustice, there seems to be no escaping from the oppression of bad leaders who subject their people to the power of false gods and deceive them by false pretences, and he asks: "Why are the deceivers powerful?" (44,20). Sometimes dismay takes on the form of despair: "To what land shall I turn? Where bend my steps?" (46,1), and leads to a question about the future: "When shall this rotten mass of lies dissolve?" (48,10).

These verses clearly constitute a moving testimony of Zarathustra's existential drama, of his searching for answers (see Part I). To summarise, Zarathustra admired the incredible beauty of nature and was dazzled by starry night skies, by the shining of the sun and moon. He was touched by nature's ingenuity and the fact that everything is in constant motion. Though barely affected by wonder and admiration, he was awakened by the scream of mother earth, and a growing concern took shape in him. The primal scream attributed to mother earth can be read as a call for help from his deeper self, from the unfathomable texture of life. His solitary quest was expressed through the voice of the "soul of the earth" that goes so far as to ask "Why did you create me?" (29,1). Soul-searching and anxiety of abandonment, anguish and desolation, often characterises the longing for kind and loving relationships.

Zarathustra was in fact deeply affected by the idleness and inability of his contemporaries to understand the world in which they live. The people surrounding him did not seem to share his sense of admiration for nature's splendid beauty. He deplored the disrespect towards life's splendor and was even under the impression that the life of the people around him unfolded in darkness. As if they were dead, living in an equally sepulchral world. Once he had been enlightened by an inner eye, Zarathustra was overwhelmed by the beauty of nature, astonished by the brilliant interplay between all things, by the enchantment he experienced in the ingenious composition of the universe. We recognise in his descriptions the philosophical amazement at the existence of things, rather than at their non-existence, together with the search for suitable answers in many of his darkest moments.

Discerning mind

From the very first verses of the *Gathas*, Zarathustra explored the depths of his own consciousness. He questioned widely-accepted ideas, the meaning of life, and he searched for a reference point in the continuous coming and going of hesitations. Almost like Descartes, he was subject to doubts and wondered whether any element could resist the human intellect when it is overeager to discover the ultimate truth, overeager to overcome fears through distortions of the mind. As a matter of fact, in one passage of the *Gathas*, he highlighted the importance of the discerning soul (31,3), and developed this highly original vision according to which it is essential to distinguish and clarify things. A discerning mind recognises the obstacles to thinking and has the capacity to discover hidden connections between the way of thinking and the things in the world. This way, the enlightenment of the consciousness thanks to different intensities of light is emphasised. The light metaphor – next to the fire symbolism – is indeed a central element in Zoroastrian culture (see Part II).

The discerning mind refers to the ability of the mind that allows us to distinguish between different strata of light and darkness. Therefore, the organ of vision acquired at birth and functioning, is to be activated and put to an effective use. Learning how to discern and differentiate is essential in the process of widening our consciousness. It represents a major ability in this proto-philosophy, also in coping with the many manifestations of deceit, especially when the human intellect is struggling to accept reality. In the interest of more truthfulness to come, Zarathustra highlighted this element that no one can counterfeit: human deception is limited in the face of infinite wisdom which cannot be deceived (45,4).

To proceed from darkness to light is a well-known metaphor in the process of enlightenment. It implies that we begin by taking notice of our own inconsistencies. In order to ensure that awareness is not reduced to a momentary illusion that leaves no mark on reality, we take care "to weigh each word carefully" (30,2). The act of discernment enables a person not to allow indifference to have the upper hand and to cast new light on things. According to the different degrees of understanding, existence can be designated in terms of the brighter and the darker side. The discerning mind enables us to learn from our mistakes and to see the act of 'free choice' as a way of progressing, of renewing our perspective, and as a chance to adjust our way of life.

Similarly, in the *Republic*, Plato defined the act of discernment as the "universal cause of all righteousness and all beauty" (517b). The discerning soul is symbolised by an enlightenment of the consciousness, of the human mind residing in a world of shadows, but discovering different intensities of light. Plato's metaphor of the cavern, of souls chained in darkness, was actually a vision inspired by the Orient, stemming from the first civilisations in the East. This cannot be emphasised enough. The Greek philosophers, who admired Zarathustra, were impressed by this view of reality. Today, we may even claim that Western thinking adopted the symbolism of light and darkness, even to a point that is has barely developed otherwise than in terms of light and darkness. What is crucial in this respect is that the two opposites of light and darkness are not mutually exclusive. Zarathustra – like Krishna or Buddha – underlined the fundamental importance of both to awaken human potential.

So, the organ of vision that functions passively, can be activated to be used effectively in our learning how to discern and differentiate. This is essential in the process of deepening our intuition and awareness, stimulating our self-development, opening up our minds and hearts to the beauty of the world, developing our responsiveness and widening our social abilities. Intelligent, well-formed ideas are the result of a patient unravelling of the different layers of the mind. As a substrate, they form a good basis for acting thoughtfully. Good thinking was already a high form of doing for Zarathustra; it means we can actually take notice of what is brought to our attention. Ill-considered thoughts, then, also have a function inasmuch as they help us see more clearly round the cunning bends of the mind.

Nature's order

We can certainly identify an ecological philosophy or ecosophy in these teachings. In Part V, I address the question whether the ecology of wisdom that is developed here could possibly offer direction in the current ecological urgency; whether the metaphor of light recurrently shining in the darkness is a line of thought that still remains valid. As we shall see, light, fire and warmth are central elements in Zoroastrian culture; they are practically archetypical features, inherent to all humanity. Fire has a highly symbolic meaning when the inner flame participates in the universal fire. The beneficial effect of light and fire is to be consolidated by and in the human mind and heart. It cannot simply be passively consumed. To respond to light and fire requires a response-ability in a giving relationship.

Indeed, the exposure to light or fire in a passive, one-way relationship does not automatically have the beneficial effect of opening up to connectivity. This misinterpretation leaves out the fact that what is life-giving should also be nourished in the life-giving process itself. The relationship between energy sources and energy receivers must be an interactive one if it is to endure. Therefore, the so-called 'worship' of light and fire should be taken seriously, and not simply be reduced to the eager consumption of beneficial effects. It is a deep-rooted idea of the West to equate the admiration of wisdom in pre-rational cultures with the adoration of the physical sun, to misjudge pre-rational practices of worship as an honouring of the physical sun, of light and fire.

Now, Zarathustra's idea of making choices that are beneficial to evolution originated in times when humanity accepted the idea of fatalism and that individuals were resigned to being subjugated to destiny or bad fate. He formulated possible outlines of a future in which humans have a say in what happens to them. He dreamt of future generations becoming aware of the possibility of developing a discerning mind, who refuse to copy bad habits and understand their potential of outgrowing irresponsible actions. The responsible human beings he had in mind reflect upon the extent to which freedom can play a part in making the world a better place. So he encouraged his companions to devote particular attention to nature's way and develop themselves in accordance with nature's order. Also, to pay attention to what is so generously made available.

Zarathustra, once moved by the beauty of the world, presented life as as a process of participating in a well-ordered universe. Struck by the beauty of nature, he considered beautiful things as reflecting a natural order. Beauty affected him to such an extent that it inspired him to be more open to hidden relationships, to the hidden relationships between what can be seen and what cannot be seen. His sensitive soul, inspired by the marvels of nature and its vulnerability, harboured a determination to protect and ensure its durability. Things that enchant the human heart can in fact trigger the desire to protect them and make them last. As a reaction to the primal scream, Zarathustra claimed: "mother earth has been created to bring joy" (47,3).

In short, this boiled down to holding integrity as something valuable worth striving for, possibly leading to a happier life. Zarathustra assured his companions that no relief would come from false promises and self-deception. In fact, anyone who guides his thoughts, words, and actions, and is moved by the wish to make them correspond, might by this attitude alone find appropriate responses. Otherwise stated, the universal problem of honesty and falsehood was addressed by him thanks to the magical, secret links that emerge once in a while. It enables humans to intuitively make connections between living beings and cosmic dynamism (see Part III).

Let us be clear that the 'universal' dimension implied in the *Gathas* concerned first and foremost the brotherhood and that it was implemented on a very small scale. Then, especially in the later verses, there is an evolution towards a growing community. There are references to "all those who help (...) mother earth" (51,3); "lead us into light" (51,16); "teach unto the living" (51,19); "within us" (51,20); individuals who "make of every act an act of worship" (51,22); "our happy flock" (53,8). In the different translations, the plural has given way to the more global term of 'mankind', thereby putting the potential of universalisability in the foreground.

Eyes of the heart

The chanted verses, known as the *Gathas*, fortunately provide us with the thoughts of this existential thinker[8]. They took the form of mantras, sung in an old idiom, close to Vedic Sanskrit, today also called Old Avestan or Gathic[9]. Most of the Avestan knowledge was committed to writing under the Persian Sasanian rule (from the 3rd to the 7th century AD)[10]. A sophisticated alphabet of 48, in some instances 53 signs, was designed for the purpose[11]. A translation in French of the Avestan texts was first published in the late 18th century. Worth mentioning is the fact that no distinction was made between the *Gathas* of Zarathustra and the *Avesta*. It took the orientalists almost a century to correct this misconception.

The *Gathas* have been transmitted orally through the ages, initially by the companions of Zarathustra, the Magi, who migrated from East Iran to

---

8   We should treat the data of the transmission with caution. According to Dastur Maneckji Nusservanji Dhalla, Hermippus of Smyrna (3rd century BC) studied the two million verses of Zarathustra and he refers to the Arab historians Tabari and Masudi who are said later to have transcribed the Avestan texts on two hundred pieces of animal skin. Dhalla maintains that two copies of Avestan texts that had been ordered by the king Vishtaspa – mentioned in the *Gathas* – had been transported to the library Dizh-i-Nipisht and Ganj-i-Shipigan. One copy was confiscated by Alexander the Great and translated into Greek. Theopompus of Chios (4th century BC) and Hermippus are believed to have had access to these texts, after which Plutarch (1st century AD) rediscovered the lost work of Zarathustra. See also Phiroz Nasarvanji Tavaria, *A Manual of Khshnoom: The Zoroastrian Occult Knowledge* (Bombay, Parsee Vegetarian and Temperance Society and Zoroastrian Radih Society, 1971).

9   Old Avestan was spoken in the second millennium BC and Younger Avestan in the first millennium BC. Old Avestan, close to Vedic Sanscrit, is an Old Iranian language, together with Old Persian that is several centuries younger. Under Parthian rule, the knowledge in Old Avestan composing the *Avesta*, was written in Pahlavi (Middle Persian), a language descended from Old Persian, the language of the Achaemenids.

10 Koenraad Elst maintains that the Zoroastrian tradition was written down in the Christian age (Arsacide and Sasanian periods) and especially after the beginning of Muslim rule between the 7th and the 9th centuries". 'The conflict between the Vedic Aryans and Iranians', *Indian Journal of History and Culture* (Chennai, Autumn 2015).

11 According to Khosro Khazai, the Avestan texts were transcribed by the Parthians in Pahlavi, using only consonants. He observes that it was in the third century AD, during the Sasanian Empire, that an alphabet was developed that included the vowels and phonetic accents. *Les Gathas: Le livre sublime de Zarathoustra* (Paris : Albin Michel, 2011, p. 42).

the West (see Part IV). A most notable contribution was that of generations of Zoroastrian priests who learned the 238 verses by heart, which even today are chanted in Zoroastrian temples. Over the ages, these age-old verses sung as mantras lost part of their initial meaning, probably because of the appeasing effect of the recitation. Although they were thought-provoking from the very beginning, and were composed as replies to unbearable injustices, they were transmitted during many centuries through sound and repetitive rehearsal. Ritual chanting can be performed as a way of revitalising a commitment and of reinforcing our trust in the events. In Zoroastrian festivities, Avestan verses accompany the rituals carried out with great care. To Zoroastrians, it is a way of re-living the experience of Zarathustra, who invited his listeners to open up to the "eyes of the heart".

In my opinion, what is to be highlighted is the potential of the human mind and heart to open up; it is the disclosure of the "eyes of the heart" that is emphasised in several verses. This expression properly translates the meeting of wisdom and love, that manifests itself as much in the mind as it does in the heart; as much in the desire to know more about the world as it does in the way of life. If half of the *Gathas* is formulated in the form of responses, their revelatory character can be interpreted as a manifestation of the initial scene of human conscience. These hymns are not just statements or announcements by an individual who gives expression to his existential quest, they also function as opening chants. They are speculative, mental exercises, most of them very uplifting, and their recitative power, sung as mantra's, can provoke a transfer of energy.

The expression "eyes of the heart", which by the way survived in Sufism, reflects the opening of the mind to the inner universe. Most important is this opening to the space within and to good thinking. Mental exercises and intuitive understanding are most welcome when they are carried out in search for right answers, for earnest guidelines; when we cannot remain captive, deaf and blind to the yearning of the 'soul of mother earth'. What really matters is the act of responding to the inner call understood in terms of an invitation to see the wider picture and attempts to make our acts correspond with a demand coming from elsewhere. Through good thinking, we may hope to gain knowledge of nature's order (30,8).

When these verses first appeared in the West in the 18th century, however, European scholars felt compelled to emphasise a difference in approach. On the one hand, there is the thought-provoking aspect of the verses; on the other hand, the worshipping function of the hymns, since they are chanted as songs of despair or songs of praise. Till this day, one of the key issues debated by European scholars concerns these different approaches. Christian Bartholomae, in his translations, stressed that there is a learning process implied in Zarathustra's teachings, in what he called the sermons of Zarathustra (1905). While Helmut Humbach, in his translations, privileged the worshipping function of these hymns of praise (1959). His collegue Jean Kellens followed the same line of interpretation, by putting the main emphasis on the ritual practice of Zoroastrians.

Kellens also mentioned the fact that a Western issue was introduced into an Eastern religion, by maintaining that the reception of the *Gathas* by scholars with a Protestant background (Haug, Geldner, Bartholomae) indirectly promoted the interpretation of Zarathustra as a 'reformer', comparable to the Protestant reaction to the power of the Roman Catholic church[12]. But more recently, the reduction of the *Gathas* to a liturgical recitative and to an exclusive function of rite has been contradicted by scholars like Antonio Panaino and Amir Ahmadi[13]. We can actually observe a cleavage in the interpretation of Zoroastrianism and the debate will surely continue to bring new arguments to support one view or the other.

Response-ability

Zarathustra's companions were encouraged to think for themselves and in case of doubting, to postpone decision-making. Obviously, Zarathustra did not encourage indecision. Doubting is fundamental, but only as a means, not as a goal. He thus proposed to reflect on how we react to things. Indeed, a reaction is not the same as a response, especially when it is impulsive and leaves no room for a reflective interval. When things happen, it is important that we create a distance with our immediate thoughts. As we are immersed in a situation, an extended mental space is created thanks to an imaginary displacement in the position of a spectator. We postpone

---

12   Jean Kellens, 'L'Avesta, Zoroastre et les sources des religions indo-iraniennes' (www.clio.fr, 2004). Kellens is also the author of *Zoroastre et l'Avesta ancien. Quatre leçons au Collège de France* (Louvain-Paris, Peeters, 1991).

13   Amir Ahmadi, *The Daeva Cult in the Gathas: An Ideological Archeology of Zarathoustra* (London, Taylor & Francis, 2015). And Antonio C.D. Panaino, *Rite, parole et pensée dans l'Avesta ancien et récent* (Vienna, Verlag der Österreichischen Akademie der Wissenschaften, 2004).

our immediate reactions and make use of our faculty to think – the act of thinking implying a series of considerations and reflections, as in a mirror.

We thus make room for the inner universe and for what happens, and we pay attention to what enters our mind. This is how Zarathustra found a means, a tool to determine the extent to which humans act in accordance with the order of nature. He succeeded in enhancing our response-ability by inventing the 'tripartite motto' and drew attention to our inner inconsistencies, to the distance between our thoughts, words and deeds. As we shall see, he encouraged his companions to face up to the denial of this distance between saying and doing. He urged them to recognise the structural divide between thought, words and action on a micro-scale as a way of discovering the hidden order on a macro-scale. From then on, to try to make thinking, speaking and acting correspond was presented as a rule of life.

According to this arch-practice, a responsive mind enhances the capability to respond appropriately. Especially when something unforeseen occurs, the ability to respond enhances our readiness and openness towards otherness. And it may imply a co-responsiveness in the making of better choices. The further developed 'love of wisdom' or *mazdaphilia,* begins with a task to be achieved: "With discernment, each one of you, with an informed mind, will weigh the highest truths" (30,2). My suggestion to give this proto-philosophy the name of 'mazdaphilia' is intended to distinguish it from Ancient Greek philosophy as a discipline.

The Indo-European word *mazda*, a symbol of wisdom, is the equivalent of the Greek word *sophia*. In Greek, the term 'philosophy' means love (*philia*) of 'wisdom' (*sophia*). Derived from the combination of Indo-European and Greek roots, the neologism mazdaphilia refers to Zarathustra's proto-philosophical love of wisdom. Of course, it emerged during the period generally defined as archaic and differing from Greek philosophy because it is pre-disciplinary and most intuitive of nature. Naturally, the *ante litteram* philosophical thoughts were not analytical or critical; neither were they epistemological or ontological. They touched upon the daily practice, upon a specific way of life.

Mazdaphilia primarily reflects a way of life, a holistic knowledge that is put to practice. Its basic value, striving for consistency in life, is as important as contemplative love of wisdom or thought-through reflections.

No love of wisdom is worthy of its name if it does not manifest itself as much in thought as it does in the way of being. True, the expression mazdaphilia is maybe less deterritorialised than 'philosophia'. Still, next to the development of good thinking, it reflects the striving for wisdom-in-act, a way of life that can become a social practice. After all, this was how Zarathustra connected the mind and the heart and discovered a secret order between our thoughts and our words, between our words and our deeds. He suspected that humans become more human when they open up to their thoughts and deeds, and pay attention to what happens to them when they get trapped in the cunning mind.

In my previous publication in French on Zoroastrianism, I emphasised the universal dimension of the *Gathas*. My suggestion was to present mazdaphilia as a universalisable way of life, based on the existential aspects present in these verses. Some readers saw it as a secular version of the religion, while others believed that mazdaphilia could well exist next to religious and non-religious ethics, thus leaving sufficient space for contemplation or community building. In the present publication, I underline the philosophical aspect of these verses and present it as a practical philosophy, as an arch-practice that can be revived in our multilingual societies. From this viewpoint, the notion *arch-practice* might be preferable to mazdaphilia.

PART ONE
HOW?

Responding to injustices

The cautious activism we find in the *Gathas* is a characteristic of Zarathustra's indignation when confronted with human irresponsibility. He was particularly concerned about injustices perpetrated by individuals who see others as a source of exploitation and gain. It made him feel as though his mission was to liberate the oppressed people around him, especially since they were not even aware of their subjection. So, he tried to make people realize they were being exploited. He tried to stir their consciences so they would become aware of the deceitful attitudes of their leaders. Zarathustra's first concern was the danger that is faced by honest individuals, who live among the followers of deceit that favour the path of least resistance.

Throughout the *Gathas*, Zarathustra engaged in a fight against injustices. His reflections proceeded slowly in accord with the rhythm of his questioning. He assured his listeners that they could become responsible beings if they refused to be fooled by those who take advantage of their good belief; that they too are capable of evaluating the meaning of a lifetime spent in deceiving oneself and misleading others. He told them of his own experience: the more he encountered hypocrisy, the more he contested the oppression of the people, determined as he was not to turn a blind eye on injustices. Nevertheless, he had to avoid making the same mistakes himself. How can one fight injustice without falling into the trap of causing even more injustice?

Zarathustra understood it is not enough to accuse false leaders and teachers who poison the people's minds out of self-interest or take advantage of their credibility. Above all, he encouraged his audience to question their inclination to follow false leaders and to believe false promises made by individuals driven by the prospect of personal gain or profit. He confronted his followers with their own tendency to give free rein to injustice. In other words, even though they were oppressed, they themselves were inclined to abuse and deceive. Most remarkable is that the ancient Iranian thinker did not promise to liberate them from injustice. What he did was directly address their potential to transform whatever conditioned them.

The importance of being responsive to injustices already appears in the first *Gatha*: "There is no authority in the world that can suppress injustice. I know of no one who protects the just from the unjust" (29, 3), says one of the characters in the opening act. Indeed, nobody but the humans themselves can save humanity from falsehood and misconduct. This means the resistance has to come from themselves: the resistance against the merchant spirit, against greed and gain which empoison the spirit of fairness. No one will ever ban injustices, but the killers for profit can be stopped. Although they trick others into things they do not want, and "can obtain prosperity and fame [...], the eternal principle of trueness prevails" (32,6).

In this chapter, all of the attention turns to the useful instruments Zarathustra offered which enable us to dedicate ourselves to right-mindedness, to resist to injustices rather than become unjust ourselves. In the confrontation with injustices, it becomes clear that unmasking our own cheating and pretending serves to "increase dedication in the heart" (48,1).

False leaders

Several recommendations can be found in the *Gathas* with regard to the "encouragement of the heart" and to a life in accordance with dedication and truth (49,5). On several occasions, Zarathustra warned against joining the earth's great ones who boost the hunger for power and trick people to "leave the path of honest work" (32,12). He denounced false leaders who take advantage by cheating and making false promises; who, in order to exploit the credulity of people, resort to demagogy and false arguments, having only their own gain in mind. Hypocrites and demagogues find pleasure in distorting reality, all the more so if they consider this pleasure to be harmless and well-intentioned. What bothered Zarathustra in particular was the brainwashing carried out by educated men and the indoctrination of bad leaders to defeat others. "Corrupt religious leaders trick people and support oppressive and malevolent rulers" (48,10). Religious fanatics make up stories and tell others how to gain the favour of the gods.

Part One. How?

To those who are guided by false powers and pervert the working of the good, Zarathustra addressed these words: "You, cheaters with treacherous thoughts [...], from your self-centred minds do all your double-dealing actions spring" (32,3). He accused them of being the cause of moral decline: "With your tricks and false promises you trick all of humanity" and you mislead the "duped who have accepted the supremacy of deceit". In a tone most severe, he reprimanded the cheaters who "promise greatness on earth for those who do not follow trueness" (32,5). And those, who at the service of false gods, "blinded by pride, made deaf by teachings false, princes and priests would like to yoke mankind to evil deeds and thus destroy true life" (46,11).

He advised all of them: "What true and lasting progress might imply, this can be learnt from life on earth alone" (32,7). Fortunately, Zarathustra did not only pile up the accusations, nor did he insist they take on another identity, become someone else, someone they are not. He first attacked the cheating part in the cheater. Rather than judging and identifying a person as a deceiver, one finds in the *Gathas* a proposition to fight the "deceit in the deceiver" (44,14). This implies that an individual can become aware of the degree of deception present in his words and deeds, and personally engage in a durable fight against a bad habit; and moreover, also thus engage in a fight against those who try to destabilise others.

Zarathustra observed that "the fickle person has a twisted image of the correct path" (51,13). In his opinion, ignorance and cowardice are the source of the twisted mind that produces a distortion of the facts. Malicious deceit being based on a distortion of reality requires proportional resistance and perseverance. What is remarkable is that Zarathustra, in those days already, addressed some very important questions. How to make others understand that false teachers "twist what is true" and despise honest individuals? When they act as if they did not have the opportunity to develop their own selves. How can one tolerate disrespectful people and, paradoxically, their ignorance? If they do not realize what is wrong in what they do, they will continue to take advantage of others who remain defenceless.

Resistance

Corrupt leaders resort to misuse of intellect, not through ignorance, but through shrewdness: "The perverted mind leads to such confusion that those who act in the worst way become the favourites" (32,4). Like no other before him, Zarathustra was particularly sensitive to the fact that man at birth has a reason or intellect that he is free to develop, but which he ultimately transforms into an instrument of self-deception. He understood that reflection is an incredible tool in the motivation of valuing one's own ego, of shining before everyone else. Either humans see themselves as inferior and need a boost of self-confidence, or they believe others are fools who can be trapped by their cunning. Indeed, through hypocrisy, bad leaders present themselves as superior beings, when in fact they are actually concealing their own inferiority. Corrupt leaders knowingly transform reality and profit from people's ignorance, while they have only the pursuit of their own well-being in mind. Premeditated deception is typical of the power hungry and it is mainly a mimetic attitude.

Zarathustra noted that, sadly, people are easily deceived by signs of affluence in men of power. Ordinary people who are lacking in education or critical thinking will take everything they say at face value. This way, words can become terrifying weapons, not to mention the abuse of power that goes along with it. Twice hypocritical are the men of power who want to keep the people in ignorance, who deny them an education, and who will do anything to keep them in their grip. Hypocritical behaviour is then passed on from one individual to the next; and the more individuals there are that adopt this kind of behaviour, the more individuals there will be who will have to conceal that they are not equal to their ideas. Even the rectifier of wrongs, when he acts like a learned judge, can become a concealer of his own inability to live according to the rules he decrees.

"The false prevent the righteous everywhere from helping man along the upward path" (46,4), observed Zarathustra with regret. At first, most discouraging was his lonesome fight in denouncing the malpractices which allowed the deceivers to continue their bad habits. Rather than to cultivate the readiness to listen to the inner voice, the power-hungry hardly realized what they have at their disposal. They behaved as if they were deprived of conscience and instead of protecting the beauty of their environment, they committed senseless and criminal acts. So, if Zarathustra denounced the "leading oppressors allied with religious chiefs who try to dominate the people by ruse and force" (46,11), it was equally crucial that more people detected the fact that they were being exploited. If not, the abuse of power could affect the whole community, especially if no one addressed the root of the problem.

In order to measure a person's ability to stand up to the power-hungry who invent all sorts of techniques to secure the submission of the people, Zarathustra discovered an interesting instrument. It allowed those who chose to resist to be ready not only to lose the advantages that come from entertaining privileged contacts with the powerful, but also to risk adversity and its consequences. In his existential and sociological quest, Zarathustra discovered a way of confronting one's own attraction to power and to determine whether one's relations are ego-centred or based on respect. Thanks to the invention of the tripartite motto, he could end his relationship with liars and overcome his initial hesitation, and stated: "I consider myself first and foremost to be dedicated to the good and the enemy of the followers of the lie" (43, 8).

As is explained further, true acts are based on the three modes of human action: thinking, speaking, acting. Zarathustra claimed that "he who listens to what is most true and does so throughout his life, restores the wisdom inside of him" (31,19). Thanks to the tripartite motto, he discovered a way of durably resisting untrueness and of promoting a life dedicated to trueness. So, in his opposition to false leaders, he addressed his listeners and explained they pretend to be virtuous men, but lead a life of lies in secret. He told them that they hope to escape themselves the wrath of the gods; they appear to be just towards the gods, while being unfair towards humankind. "These leaders should not be falsely complemented" (43,15), so he urged his followers. It is better not to flatter them, since flattery allows the deceiver to continue to delude himself.

Daring to reflect

Zarathustra made no false promises to liberate the human mind of the inclination to be untrue. In his vision, to dare to reflect means to dare to question and to probe one's own motivations. It means learning how to change one's perspective and learning about one's capacity to progress on the journey to more trueness. It means to dare to show confidence in one's own abilities, in the renewal of one's forces to be better prepared to resist in the future. As we shall see, it is not enough to think in terms of the truth or the lie; what we need to understand is that to speak and to act are two different things, and that we can choose in advance which action we give in to. According to Zarathustra, relations that fail to be accompanied by in-depth thought and by a corresponding way of being do not produce the beneficial effect of the true act.

We recognise in this that feigning honesty in order to mislead is equal to making bad use of our faculty to think. We probably believe this will not have an incidence on our lives and that of others, but we deceive ourselves. More regularly than we wish to admit, we neglect the fact that we can actually confront old habits. These could be of a rather inoffensive nature such as dishonesty, but also include a wider range of deception. A white lie, for instance, is admissible, when we wish to prevent hurting someone unnecessarily. But false testimony and perjury go way beyond casual insincerity[1]. Not to resist the inclination to deceive can degenerate into more serious misuse and violations. One of the most underestimated traps of human reflection is to allow oneself to cross the line between innocent lying and fraudulent acting, to give in to the corruption of the mind.

Zarathustra suggested his interlocutors pay attention to their daily choices and advised them to think carefully before speaking and to think about the consequences of their words. He recommended: "Consult your wisdom and evaluate your thoughts, words and actions" (53,2). This invitation to evaluate the distance between saying and doing is a recurring theme in these hymns. It is a well-known fact that we tend to adapt the reality of things to our understanding or will. When we speak, we use the words that come first hand, and live in the illusion that we can verbally control reality. But words and reality are not the same thing.

The key to address our inconsistencies, according to Zarathustra, is to reflect on the distance between what we think and the words we use to express our thoughts, and also between our ideas and the world. The reader of the *Gathas* who becomes acquainted with the way we use language discovers a powerful tool that allows us to express ourselves and to communicate with each other. So, when we pay more attention to this, we also become more aware of the transformation of the elements of distortion and of what can be called the misuse of the intellect. The general idea is to arrive at this guiding principle: to be committed and to try to be honest with yourself can lead to a better social life. When a person decides to take sincerity as a guideline, the beneficial effect is that it can become a shared value.

---

1   There is no hierarchical distinction to be found in the Gathas between dishonesty, misleading, or more serious misdeeds and degrees of crimes.

Sapere aude, daring to reflect, can be summarized as follows. First of all, Zarathustra urges his audience to discover two opposite tendencies – a friend and a foe – inside themselves. Secondly, he offers a reasonable possibility to address the internal struggle, namely through the daily application of the tripartite motto. Thanks to this motto, humanity has received an instrument to individually measure our attraction to power. It allows us to determine whether our thoughts are induced by power-hunger or by respect. Thirdly, the freedom of choice involved in this daily practice is based on the understanding of the 'primordial choice'. Each context demands the renewal of one's commitment to the tripartite motto.

Two tendencies

The *Gathas* transmit this unique idea we can all put into practice. Zarathustra makes us realise that awareness of the inner struggle between the two opposite tendencies is half the job done. As a true psychologist, he explains how we can fight self-deception. This requires that we recognise the existence of two opposite tendencies inside ourselves. In Yasna 46 he shows how we can discover a tendency towards more trueness and a tendency towards being untrue. These two opposite tendencies are constantly at work in our thinking and acting. In the eyes of Zarathustra, the internal conflict between the two tendencies functions like an existential motor. Human beings who recognise this, come to term with their own inconsistencies and understand that no individual corresponds to whom he thinks he is. We are all of us the stage of an internal struggle, but we do not identify with it.

The innovative psychological element is the establishment of a close relationship with and between the two tendencies. It is not a reconciliation that is being aimed at, since the human mind easily forgets inaccurate behavior and needs to be constantly reminded. Neither is it the elimination of one of the two tendencies that is being pursued, because both are needed in the process of recognising which is the more valuable. The discovery of each of them will first require a fight against denial and the involvement of the "eyes of the heart". Above all, it depends on the determination "to live a life that is not full of lies, but a truthful life" (34,15).

So, we must acknowledge that we are all constantly under the influence of the *druj*, a Gathic word referring to falsehood, the origin of deceit and of malevolent acts. The word *druj* – the root of the German word *Betrug* –

refers to intentional misleading, to fallacious reasoning, and by extension to the intention of feigning to be another person, to the perversion of reality. Zarathustra noted that the *dregvant*, the enemy of trueness, is continuously falling into the traps of thought. What may in his eyes appear futile is far from being so, and he asked his audience: "Among the one who follows the path towards trueness and the one who follows the path towards untrueness, who has chosen the right path?" (31,18). Instead of using their intellect unwisely, as do those who have power over others, Zarathustra assured it is possible to resist the tendency towards untrueness.

The reader may have noticed that I make use of a new terminology in this book to designate the contradictory polarity (see Part III). The fact is I believe this new terminology is preferable to the usual translation of 'truth' as opposed to 'the lie'. By using the concepts trueness, as opposed to untrueness, the association with verbal statements is avoided. Also, the word 'tendency' suits the implicit movement towards more or less trueness. Thirdly, we do not present a true life as a continuous consistent life, but as a life directed towards being truthful, orientated towards what is closer to a true life and thus further away from an untrue life. It was only after a long period of reflection that I was finally convinced I had pinned down the dynamic orientation implicit in this new presentation.

To think in terms of tendencies prevents us from associating the two poles of 'the truth' and 'the lie' with static concepts like 'good' and 'bad'. This alternative terminology is useful inasmuch as it makes it possible to avoid confusion with regard to habitual translations of 'good' and 'evil', which suggest the existence of evil as such, as a negative copy of goodness as such. Unlike platonic, independent ideas, that seem to live a life of their own, the two tendencies arise in the mental world and in our interaction with the outside world. They are mutually dependent categories of the human mind, rather than autonomous entities as such.

Tripartite motto

It is of the utmost importance that we recognise these two opposite tendencies within us, one of which is emancipatory and progressive, while the other is possessive and immobilising. The first one is directed towards the human being's initial goal in the world, that is, towards the fulfilment of the individual, in the evolution towards the completion of the cycle initialised in singular conditions. This tendency alone undeniably leads to a truer life. It cannot be falsified. It concerns "the renewal of our life" (46, 19). The other tendency gives the impression that delusion is tolerable or even, that it constitutes proof of intelligence. It creates the impression that self-deception is commendable, whereas it actually traps us further within a world in which deception is perceived as something insignificant.

To discover which tendency gets the upper hand, Zarathustra relied on the tripartite motto: "good thoughts, good words, good deeds" (45,8). With the 'eyes of the heart' he understood that humans recognise the self-regulating principle and develop more wisdom thanks to this tripartite motto. It is part of the daily Zoroastrian practice that comes in the form of three registers that are taken into consideration during self-examination. Each person finds out for himself if they can admit not to always align their actions with their words. This requires courage and the ability to be open-minded. Through the motto "thinking well, speaking well, acting well" – an equivalent translation of the more common "good thoughts, good words, good deeds" –, each individual can measure the structural distance between thought, words and action. Every single person can experiment with this, and especially those individuals who pretend not be submitted to it.

Now, the structural divide between the three elements invites us to enter into a cosmic play. A crucial step is to let light spread to the darkest part of our most intimate thoughts and to open up to our inner confidant without fear of being judged. Even though it is not easy to recognise the divide between thought, words and action, the tripartite motto can become a powerful tool in the process of learning to know oneself better. Zoroastrians value this tripartite motto through permanent existential choices, like a sort of rule for life which they hold in high regard.

Most beneficial is the true power that stems from overcoming old habits that are not favourable to our social lives. Each time we recognise the motive power of this motto, it enables us to follow a good constellation in order not to get lost in the universe of opinions. In maintaining it as a personal rule of life, it can also be beneficial in social relationships. Of course, its beneficial effect is not the goal, but it is liable to nourish new attempts to make thoughts, words and deeds correspond. The readiness to follow the tripartite motto stems from a hidden understanding that there must be a link between the microcosm and the macrocosm. In fact, in the renewal of its energising potential, in the dynamics of this microcosm we can recognise the macrocosmic dynamism in miniature. Most revelatory are the moments when the constellation of the macrocosmic universe seems to be reflected in the microcosmic universe.

As an indicator to guide existence, the tripartite motto reflects the constant freedom of choice with regard to our thoughts, words and actions. Ideally, they correspond, but because the human being cannot succeed at this without some direction, the motto works as a line of vision. Understandably, it becomes useless when we reduce it to an imposed law or instruction that we blindly follow. It is not an instruction or command, let alone an order to think well, speak well, act well! Make no mistake: in the act of "thinking well, speaking well, acting well", it is indeed the readiness to make these elements correspond that is crucial. This involves an openness to try and reduce the divide between the three, which makes it the driving force behind human behaviour.

Primordial choice

Yasna 30 explains that the two tendencies are present in each individual and in each initiative, and that during a disagreement, it falls to the wisest person to choose, while the most ignorant does not choose (30,3). This passage is clear: it is not a question of choosing between two possibilities, generally thought of as a choice between good and bad. The text is about a choice and a non-choice. Not choosing for the supremacy of the first tendency equals choosing not to choose, and to give free rein to the second tendency. According to Zarathustra, choosing not to choose goes back to not involving oneself in the universal game. It means that one abstains from playing an important role. To believe that one can reduce the primordial choice to a non-choice is to separate the microcosm from the macrocosm and to retreat into one's own world.

Indeed, the individual who wishes not to perceive the two tendencies inside will also be unable to unlock his potential which will remain inactive. He will not be able to unlock the tendency towards trueness. When there is a lack of awareness of the inner struggle, he risks being lost in a counter-productive battle. This explains the necessity of pointing out in advance which side we are on: shall we join those who choose to follow the path towards trueness? It seems that in Zarathustra's opinion, an anticipated determination is the only way of falling in line with the dynamic of choosing at the moment we are taken off guard.

This demands further explanation. Every human being can discover the effectiveness of the tripartite motto, thanks to which complex situations can be faced. So, before choosing one of two paths towards trueness or deception, we take time to inspect our relationship with ourselves, the world, with others. We reflect on what the preliminary choice to daily choices signifies. If we choose a life in trueness, we understand the importance of being on the side of trueness before all choices. We submit to the one essential choice to be a free person, to the choice before all other choices. We are aware of the fact that the counter-productive tendency will not be eliminated by this choice, but at least that it will find a resistant opponent in us.

Verse 48,4 highlights the crucial thoughts that may occur along our progress towards more determination. "He who improves his thoughts, or who deteriorates them, is the one who by actions or words improves or deteriorates the conscience in himself." To voluntarily scrutinize our conscience steers us towards more trueness, even towards truths we prefer to hide. In fact, what Zarathustra is expressing in verse 30,2 does not correspond to one truth that exists somewhere and that is waiting to be unveiled. "Each one of you, with an enlightened spirit, will weigh each truth", is an invitation to face indeterminacy.

So, before even being confronted with a choice, Zarathustra makes us measure, weigh, and take into account which one of the two tendencies within us should overcome the other. Before we can find ourselves before a choice, it is necessary to take position conceptually, to mull over in advance the difference between the two tendencies: to know if you are on the side of a constructive commitment, in a position to face an indifferent mindset, if you can handle an aggressive or impatient attitude, or have a penchant for fighting against the negative or destructive tendency. So much is clear, if a dishonest life was filling most of your life, this does not mean it is directed uniquely towards falsehood, since it can be reoriented.

Freedom of choice revised

'Free will' is a philosophical expression that traditionally refers to the freedom to choose between good and bad. In the context of Zarathustra's proto-philosophy, this free choice receives a more specific meaning. We are indeed encouraged to avoid seeing a choice as being between two elements, instead of seeing it as prioritizing one element as opposed to its contrary. We understand that Yasna 31 mentions the necessity of free choice, which sounds paradoxical. Existential freedom refers to the responsibility of seizing this necessity, when we comprehend that non-choice is in fact choosing to give free rein to the second tendency. The individual who remains indifferent to the fight between the two tendencies is exposed by his very indifference to the risk that the second tendency will get the upper hand.

"Among the one who follows the path towards trueness and the one who follows the path towards deception, who has chosen the right path?" (31,18), asks Zarathustra. The two tendencies, with each one taking an opposite direction, arise with the necessity of bringing about a choice. This installs the responsibility of free choice into us, until it eventually becomes clear that we cannot not choose and meet with the primordial choice. Before the world's beauty, only the invigorating tendency brings about protective and durable feelings while the opposite, possessive tendency stops the dynamic by keeping a stranglehold on the subject.

So the freedom to choose does not so much imply a choice between good and bad. Instead we are invited to discern what is truer with reference to the tripartite motto, or what seems to have a better chance of being and staying true, in other words, to discern the potential renewal. Free choice is well and truly the daily exercise that we are compelled to do. No one can make this choice for us, although it is we who determine the primordial choice that determines our choices. If our choices could by definition be good or bad, we would simply be robots. Fundamentally, Yasna 31 is an invitation to consistently fall in with the invigorating tendency, even if we fail to live up to it.

"Before choosing one of the two paths, each one of you weigh and balance, with an enlightened spirit, the most elevated truths", Zarathustra maintains (30,2). He draws attention to the enlightened spirit, to the freedom to choose. "With illuminated minds weigh them with care", he adds (30,2). Once more, the discernment of the two paths before any choice reflects the primordial choice. The enlightened spirit has decided in advance if it is better to choose for trueness and not to allow deception to run wild. In the end, we are not choosing between the good and the bad, we are not hesitating between telling the truth and lying. We are choosing trueness over deception.

What is highlighted is that making right choices involves the faculty of thinking and a kind of categorical imperative *avant la lettre*. Daring to think is not just about mulling over side issues, since it implies an enduring fight against what is untrue. The goal of inner reflection is not to pursue a temporary sense of freedom, but to find a way of life in which one durably engages in trueness. Freedom is not something that is available on the spot; it is an orientation we choose to adopt and should not ignore. We simply know that ensnaring others out of self-interest is not the right way to build a society where people can trust each other, where each one of us can count on the other and we mutually want what is best for each other.

At the big moment known as choice, "whether he speaks true or false, whether he speaks knowingly or not", he can "overcome his doubts by dedication" (31,12). Zarathustra speaks of persons who inspect their motivations deep down inside themselves, who examine if they are interested in power (be it social, religious or political) and to what extent they are prepared to resist it. This probably incited his companions to distance themselves from a passive vision of life, actually called 'non-life' and to consider the connection between 'life' and the course of nature. The idea of having an impact on the further development of existence enabled them to make a distinction between life and non-life.

Life and non-life

Zarathustra suggests that the two opposite tendencies help determine the moments of our existence in terms of life and non-life. "Life was made by one, the other made non-life", he observes (30,4). A difference is established between life and non-life, two Gathic expressions, typical of this *avant la lettre* psychology. Zarathustra feels self-deception is a condition of non-life. We may well have succeeded in its undertaking, but with a heavy heart. Once we remain stuck in our successes or in the over evaluation of our brief pleasures, we find that not we but the illusion of progress increases.

Zarathustra has himself experienced what he calls 'non-life'. In his opinion, we start examining ourselves in order to leave behind a 'non-life' that has become unbearable. Non-life refers to an existence that does not involve deep thought and awareness, to a life lived in ignorance and without resistance. When we experience non-life, we feel as if we have no role to play in this world and that there is no meaning to existence. This condition may lead to the inertia of a life without circumspection, recognisable moments we go through when we fail to give a direction to our existence. Once we realise this, we are tossed between the shame of desperation in the midst of all that is given to us, and the despair originating from a chain of setbacks. Either we are victims of our own thoughts or we put the blame on others.

The longer we live like dead people, the more we feel that it is too late to change and open up to what is revitalising, and the less we have any idea of the inherent potential to grow and to regenerate ourselves. By self-examination, Zarathustra discovered that the two main rivals are powerfully at work and that we can easily fall back into the traps of the counter-productive tendency. He went on searching for the most truthful one, which does not hide behind appearances and has no reason to invent pretexts. According to him, everyone is free to choose his own way of life, telling the truth, lying, or learning how to resist to bad choices. He arrived at this conclusion: "Let each one choose deeds of piety" (53,2) as the ultimate choice offering a better chance of protection against bad choices.

The ability that allows to differentiate between life and non-life depends, according to Zarathustra, on the ability to recognise the difference between the two tendencies. To link theory and practice by means of the tripartite motto is crucial and prevents giving free rein to the misleading mind. Thanks to the primordial choice, he seems to be telling us that we shall be less prone to neglect the difference between the active and the passive attitude, between living one's life and one's life being lived. Life, in its opposition to non-life, reflects the existential condition that takes place in a constant dynamic tension between the two opposite tendencies. The first tendency is regenerative and oriented towards the future, towards what has a potential of renewal. The second tendency is stagnant and encourages the individual to shut himself off from the world, thus impeding the inherent potential of self-development. This state of things is assimilated to non-life. So, when we learn how to have confidence in the flow of things, we take charge of our lives and commit to developing our potential, to grasping opportunities and to reach an equilibrium. But if we live according to what others see as being valid and blindly follow the ideas we receive from others, we are limited to the single condition of being alive, rather than feel alive and well.

To conclude, life and non-life are the concepts used in the *Gathas* referring to the kind of life we choose. They are not to be associated with life and death, nor with an afterlife, as is too often pointed out. As we shall see, Zarathustra's questioning is oriented towards the possibility of reaching the 'house of trueness' or the 'house of song'. Life in trueness is associated with reaching the 'abode of light' (31,20) – later on assimilated with 'paradise' – with the state of the individual who orients his life towards completion on the path of trueness (44,8). Whereas the non-life of the individual who is indifferent to the initial potential of a happy fulfilment is associated with the 'abode of falsehood', also translated as the 'house of deceit' or the 'house of lies', later on identified as 'hell', the state we find ourselves in when we do not resist to the power of deception (see Part III, the two abodes).

Happiness

One of the first songs of the *Gathas* begins with wishing that humans may greet "the happiness of two worlds, the bodily and the spiritual" (28,2). And some stanzas further, the issue of life in accordance with its truest form is reached (31,2). To free the world of lies and hypocrisy is one of the *Gathas*' major themes: "The false ones do not reach happiness" (51,12). One of the last verses mentions the contact Zarathustra made with the inner confidant he could trust, about putting his "perfect trust in good thinking" (53,3), which allowed him to resist falseness on a regular basis. In fact, he could not refrain from telling others of the joy that arose in moments of necessary resistance, of the joy stemming from what he experienced as the sudden correspondence of his acts and nature's order.

Plato, who admired the wisdom of Zarathustra, speaks in similar terms of the lover of wisdom: "To associate oneself with something divine and well-regulated, is to become a well-regulated being" (*Republic* 500d). The lover of wisdom, if he agrees with the divine order, will himself become ordained. To improve one's life means following the path that leads to greater happiness for all. Several statements by the great philosopher show that Plato respected Persian education and leadership, and that he shared the view of the Persian sage[2]. Like Zarathustra, Plato believed that when

---

2 For a more comprehensive research and quotations by Plato on the Persian values, I refer to my *Ainsi pensait Zarathoustra: Une philosophie avant la lettre* (Paris, Non Lieu, 2017).

man undertakes something guided by wisdom, it will lead him to happiness (*Meno*, 88b-d). Both argued that it is advantageous to learn something conscientiously and that the same applies to courage and confidence within reason, while stupidity has the opposite effect.

To Zarathustra, happiness is inscribed in a context. Human virtues are not beneficial or evil, egoistic or altruistic in themselves, but only in context. Their potential energy, stemming from the good decisions we make, has its origin in a dynamic conception of life. Happiness alike is to be activated and to be shared following the way we put our mind to use, from the viewpoints we choose. What matters is the way we take part in friendships, how the state of mind is transmitted and with possible repercussions on our future actions. As is explained further, well thought-out, considered decisions with regard to living together can find a correspondence with an intelligently designed cosmic dynamism. Potential happiness depends indeed on the benefits of open-mindedness, respect and care for the whole of creation.

In order "to make this world alive, man has been given the choice of being diligent or not" (45,9), Zarathustra stated. For humans, animals and plants to be happy and fulfilled, he found that the destabilising effects of the impression that life is made of arbitrary events must be reduced. The idea that all beings are random casualties does not indeed inspire hope. If creation makes no sense at all, if all takes place in vain, no magical energy can arise from the judicious use of our mind; from the primordial choice that things can happen for some reason. According to Zarathustra, the world of plants and animals is already perfect, while human life is imperfect. The human mind is thus conceived that it needs the full use of its potential to unravel cosmic ingenuity and to reach happiness. Whoever regards this vision on nature's dynamism as an unrealistic or preordained design, may surmise that cosmic complexity conceals its ambiguous nature. At the same time, it presents itself as an autonomous movement, while its heteronomy serves as the enabling condition for humans to make autonomous choices.

Zarathustra added that the free individual and the untrustworthy individual can expect different destinies. Thus his reply to Mazda: "The man or woman, who does bring to life what you consider best (...) will march with me across the weigh bridge" (46,10). He addressed his companions to let them know that they will embark together in the fight against deceptive and untrue thoughts, against perversions and perspectives deformed by the foe, and thus reach 'the abode of light'. Together with the friend and confidant, he assured them that "who satisfies Spitama's heart and helps Zarathustra to fulfil his task, shall gain renown as upright and true" (46,13). In doing so, they could free themselves progressively from what kept them from finding the blessing of happiness, from discovering that a free person does not cheat.

Social practice

As Plato said, the great misfortune of mankind is that wisdom and power attract each other. That they seek each other out and sometimes meet. A thousand years before the emergence of Greek philosophy[3], a virtuous man was not simply someone who had inborn qualities, but someone who had managed to develop them and make them productive; whose mental nourishment came from the circumspect handling of the tripartite motto as an instrument that functioned almost like an algorithm. In the case of Zarathustra, the possibility of developing his potential for wisdom made him not give up and cultivate a self-reliance that was beneficial to others. Maybe he was always one step behind the emergence of wise choices, but he continued to choose. Seekers of knowledge, strong in spirit, also designated as 'self-reliant' are appointed in the *Gathas* to inspire the fellow workers and the friends (32,1).

The reader of these verses comes to the finding that the clan, the family and the community were all engaged in the "fostering of life" (33,3). Each one was appointed a duty (53,4). Soon the Zoroastrian way of life had the character of a social practice within the communities, although it is more correct to speak of the social dimension this way of life held. Most probably, this dimension was limited to Zoroastrian communities in their protection against hostile individuals, against other clans. And over the years, the negative side of closed communities must even have included an unwished social control. It is difficult to speculate on this, which is why we can only refer to Zarathustra's wish to "preserve the flock and their pastures from false shepherds". As the highest servant of infinite wisdom, he tried to ward off "all ill intention": to protect "the self-reliant from thoughts that

---

3   Abtin Sassanfar expresses the regret that one can search in vain for the name of Zarathustra in the histories of philosophy: "Everything suddenly commences with the Pre-Socratic Greek schools". 'Le choix et le libre arbitre dans les « Gathas » de Zarathoustra' in *Zarathoustra et le renouveau chrétien de l'Europe* (Paris, Trédaniel, 1996, p. 126).

are perverse, the co-worker from hostile and narrow mentality, and the friend from the slanderers" (33,4).

Upon taking a closer look at the social dimension, Zarathustra was convinced that introspection by the community members would shed light on the hidden yet real motivations of their actions and have repercussions on their relationships. He who "yearns for light shall receive light" (43,2), he claimed, thus recognising a first relationship between the person who yearns for light and the source of light. And he witnessed a second relationship between persons who share the light: "Enlightenment shall come to him who shares light with others" (43,1). In the supposition that these two relations are interdependent, he could not but concede that a hidden, effective power comes from a person's openness to these kinds of relationships, from an encouraging spirit, from the readiness to renew time and time again the regenerative power of a life force that enhances the team spirit.

Zarathustra dared to make a pronouncement about what is to come: "He or she who strives to understand what is a true life ultimately carries it out" (51,19). It actually happens that a mental predisposition to trueness suddenly makes us notice the dazzling beauty of nature, waving incessantly to our hearts and minds. The engendered openness can make us notice the gap between ideas and realisation, between intention and action. It may inspire us to live in accordance with the dynamic course of real life, an issue that has forever plagued human consciousness. Of course, aspirations do not come true just by contemplating the brightness of the stars in the sky. There is no magic formula and the tripartite motto does not at all work according to the logic of cause and effect. It is not enough to achieve one of the three modalities to achieve all of them, nor is a onetime attempt effective. Underlying Zarathustra's reply, there is this one request, the repeated incitement to become a co-worker of wisdom.

A friend and a foe

A first part of the *Gathas* (28 up to 34) retraces the inner search that Zarathustra carried out during the painful moments he felt alone when he was enduring tribulations; when the fear of revealing himself was not yet balanced out by the confidence to reconfirm himself. The other part (43 up to 53) consists of possible responses when, with patience, enlightened consciousness patiently starts to free itself with entirely unforeseeable possibilities. As we will see further, Zarathustra addressed himself to the confidant inside, to infinite wisdom (Ahura Mazda) he held in the highest respect. Yasna 43 is entirely dedicated to the radiance of wisdom, while Yasna 44 highlights that the refusal of trueness offers only superficial progress.

It is clear by now that the ability to recognise the impact of the two tendencies, of the friend and the foe inside, always reconnects us with the confidence factor. By showing respect for trueness, we recognise the friend inside, namely the successful regenerator of trueness struggling against the contrary tendency. Important is to mention that the deception tendency tends to fool its opposite and wants to take over. It tries to show itself as the only valid alternative and depends on the counter-movement from which it has to draw all its energy. In fact, the difference between the two tendencies is that the first has an emancipatory dimension, while the second is a parasite and cannot regenerate by itself.

Indeed, Zarathustra sought to emancipate humanity – from anxieties and from false power – so that humans could enjoy life as it was meant to be. He believed that all men and women could think for themselves, at least if someone taught them. One of his first concerns was to free the people from fears and superstitions and to put an end to their spiritual slavery. Next, to encourage the emancipatory tendency, he explained that of the two opposite tendencies, only the one we feed can ever take the upper hand. He urged those who came in contact with the friend and the foe inside not to be indifferent and to listen to these words: "Those who choose the path of deception will not know the best existence and those who choose the way of trueness will have a better life" (30,4).

This, according to Zarathustra, means that the relationship with the foe inside has a function. Individuals who are in search of a more durable and unshakable existence and who wish to receive an orientation in life, may experience the good effect of a long-term dwelling in the nearness of true thoughts. But before anything else, they can become a friend who brings joy to others. Human warmth derives from persons who revive the universal fire and become friends with infinite wisdom and joy-bringing mother earth. "He who listens to what is most true and carries it out during his life, restores the wisdom inside of him" (31,19), was the living experience of Zarathustra. To orient one's life towards the light of trueness became his own daily choice and that of his listeners who had experienced the negative outcome of an arbitrary lifestyle.

Zarathustra thus addressed infinite wisdom: "Come to us [...] and grant to Zarathustra the joys of inner life" (28,6). Together with his companions, he must have experienced the beneficial effect of the enduring practice of the primordial choice. The brotherhood, initially the assembly of Magi, probably discovered good thinking and the long-enduring gifts of trueness. Of course, no beneficial effect can be claimed or predicted, since the idea is to engage on a daily basis in the struggle with our own inconsistencies and try not to point the finger of blame to others. Zarathustra asked infinite wisdom to support and teach his companions to become friends with infinite wisdom, and show them "how to serve our brother-man" (45,9).

The invention of confidence

In the second part of the *Gathas*, Zarathustra is under the impression that, since the good orientation entered his heart, he has actually "become more true and intelligent" (43,11). Not being constantly at the mercy of arbitrary forces, he has found a fulfilment, also in his relation to others who do the same. He has noticed that affirmative gestures like these reinforce the social fabric. And so it is that the tendency toward more trueness, based on introspection and good understanding, becomes a leading factor on the path toward more confidence. When people can rely on one another, they build a society of mutual trust. They no longer feel the need to hide behind lies and distortions that have to be maintained at all cost. By admitting they have deceived in the past, a step can be made towards a liberating movement out of a deadly form of imprisonment.

It is worth noting the confidential relationship with the friend of friends inside, as the next chapter shows. As soon as he turned towards the wiser friend inside, Zarathustra noted that "the good entered into his heart by good understanding" (43,9). In his eyes, the illusion of self-sufficiency prevents a person from apprehending a more truthful reality. When the mind and heart do not cooperate, this can lead to an unnoticed slow suicide and result in ever more deceptive reasoning. For the arising of self-confidence to be noted, a link to the process of no longer admitting self-deception is necessary. Zarathustra's explicit denunciation of self-deception is to be seen in the context of his desire to awaken those who are in doubt, so that they can start living life to the full and bring assistance to those who are "plunged into confusion" (49,1).

The wise confidant he himself turned to was Ahura Mazda, infinite wisdom, in some books designated as Wise One, All-Wise, Wisdom, or Lord Wisdom, permitting Zarathustra to open up his heart and receive the force in all its generosity. This disposition for good radiance reminds us of what Plato calls "the conversion of the soul", to turn towards the light of wisdom and allowing oneself an openness to the energy stemming from the primordial choice for trueness. For Zarathustra, it was the moment he entered in contact with the confidant he had never thought to be inside him (30,1), determined as he was in his engagement to reply to the call of mother earth.

In other words, in not denying that he was the living theatre of opposing forces, torn on both sides, his free confessional attitude had a liberating effect and it cleared a space to retreat in. In his confidential relationship with both tendencies, Zarathustra made contact with the confidant inside: "When difficulties occur, my trust in humanity guides me towards what you taught me to be and to do better: be my true self and do my best" (43,11). Can we confirm with Zarathustra that trust in the course of things grows through dedication, through the inspiration or intuition of a more authentic secret order? Trust creates, in principle, a suitable environment for self-confidence and interactions with others. It makes us internally communicate with our own strength, which dissipates unrest or confusion (53,3). In the same movement, we extend and increase our solidarity to beings in distress.

According to Zarathustra, through an adjournment of despair, each individual is able to gain greater confidence in the cosmic evolution. It is often after bad choices – as if we needed them to adjust our lifestyle – that we come in touch with our own confidant. We cultivate this relationship with life itself the way we care for a plant, a flower or a tree. It is one of the most indirect messages of the *Gathas*. Through intuition and the heart's eyes, we get a glimpse of what life on earth can mean. We dedicate ourselves to our activities and cooperate in the common project. In this sense, the idea that everything responds to a universal dynamic, to the self-regulation of trueness, on which we can rely when we enter into the cosmic play, is truly revolutionary. It makes us face up to the multiple thresholds of anxiety, instead of feeling subjugated by arbitrary laws, and teaches us to take part in a dynamic universe in which it is possible to flourish and prosper together.

PART TWO
WHO?

Iranian prophet?

The word "prophet" refers to the person who speaks by divine inspiration, as a spokesman or intermediary figure. A derivate meaning is that of the prophet who foretells and predicts the future. Both denominations have been attributed to Zarathustra, who over the centuries stood for the prophet of a Mazdean religion, an astrologer, a magician, a clairvoyant or the founder of the seven liberal arts. Over time, his name was associated with a miraculous power to change evil into good. Because of these equivocal assumptions, I have chosen to qualify Zarathustra as a thinker. Of course, he is the prophet of Zoroastrianism, a world religion to which most publications are dedicated, but it is equally important to focus on the philosophical dimension of his thinking.

The *Gathas* express the wonder that emerged in Zarathustra's heart at the beautiful way the universe is assembled. His amazement can be considered as one of the first characteristics of philosophical thought. Whether he was a reformer of anterior Mazdeism seems to be of secondary importance when one considers the new vision on life this existential thinking implies. It is clear from the *Gathas* that Zarathustra was not in favour of the worship of the ancient *daevas* and *asuras*. He rejected idolatry and regretted compulsory offerings made to demons of all kinds, and also, the sacrifices performed in order to be protected rather than to protect. This explains his attacks on the ancient gods and demons. To deceive, to cheat deliberately, consciously, out of personal interest, are assignments of "disguised monsters" (49,4), argued Zarathustra. "Their tongues only know gossip, and they have hate in their hearts" (49,4).

He thus tried to convince his audience of the deceitful character of the submission to false gods and false leaders. We will see how, according to him, the deceivers punish themselves. They humiliate and denigrate and mask reality, but they are fools and are the victims of their own ploys. They think they are deceiving others, but in reality, they are deceiving themselves. The reason why Zarathustra was so sensitive to the abuse of power by religious leaders could be found in the fact that he belonged to a family (the Spitamas) of hereditary priests for several generations. We know very little of the biography of Zarathushtra Spitama, which explains why he is sometimes considered a mythical figure, but a recent study brings evidence of the existence of Zarathustra in times as early as 1400 BC.

According to the Belgian orientalist by Koenraad Elst, a new element in the discussion on whether he was a mythical figure, just like Homer, Socrates, or Buddha, is to be found in the conflict between Vedic Aryans and Iranians. Elst concludes that "it has become entirely certain that the Iranians feature prominently in the *Rg-Veda*" and that Zarathustra "must have lived either in ca 1400 according to the Aryan Invasion Theory (AIT) or earlier". He also states that the life story of Zarathustra Spitama is not very prestigious and "sounds West-Asian". It is the "classical story of a wandering preacher who finds God during a lonely retreat". In his research, Elst characterizes Zarathustra as a spokesman of already existing communities, who became famous because of taking "the trouble of casting his ideas into poems"[1].

Companions

Zarathustra's close followers, later on known as the Magi or Persian sages, considered him an enlightened person. If the word 'enlightened' is not unequivocal, in these chapters on the prevalent role of the light metaphor, it forms a key word. The symbolic meaning of light is indeed emphasised, with reference to the brief manifestations of an illuminative source that itself remains invisible. This symbolism with an archetypical meaning is known all over the planet. Together with the plant metaphor, it is characteristic of this proto-philosophy that puts forward vision and growth as two founding elements of life.

---

1 Koenraad Elst (2015). Elst characterises Zarathustra as a court priest of the Kavi dynasty, but *kavi* means poet in Old Avestan and Old Indic, only later 'prince' or 'ruler'.

Part Two. Who?

The existence of Zoroastrian communities was unknown in the West until the 6th century BC. The Greek philosopher Pythagoras had travelled to the East, stayed in Babylon and his voyage to India made him discover a whole new universe. Influenced as he was by the oriental practice of singing mantras and invocations, the idea that reciting, repeating and chanting sacred hymns had a healing or magical effect was not unfamiliar to him. He defended the idea of a perfect order governing the universe and declared that the whole universe is ruled by the same laws. His science of numbers was a key to understanding the universe as a perfect mathematical configuration[2]. Pythagoras referred to cosmic harmony as music of the spheres that could be heard by those who understood the links between heaven and earth, and he maintained that this was within reach of all individuals, including women. Pythagoras had come to appreciate equality between men and women in Persia. He respected women and women were taken seriously in his school.

The first Greek 'philosophers of nature' saw the Magi in Asia Minor for emigrated disciples of Zoroaster. They believed Zoroaster was a contemporary thinker, living in the Western part of Persia. In the many centuries to come, the Persian thinker was known among the sages as someone who knew the secrets of existence which he was said to have revealed for the first time. To most Greek philosophers, the Magi were considered as bearers of glad tidings, bringing the message of freedom and responsibility to their interlocutors. And Zarathustra was a great wise man, whom they thought of with respect. Paul Du Breuil notes that Eudoxe of Cnides asserted that the ideas of Zarathustra penetrated the Academy of Plato and that Aristotle confirmed that these revived the spirit of the Iranian sage[3].

Before that time however, the word *magus* had received a negative connotation in Mesopotamia. By the time the Magi had reached the West, the Persian wise men were not always identified as the nomads coming

---

2   There was a Hellenistic tradition in which Zoroaster was the initiator of Pythagoras and the master of Chaldean astrologists, image that persisted till the Middle Ages and Renaissance. Robert Turcan notes that the Magi were often confused with the Chaldean culture of astrology. *Les Cultes orientaux dans le monde romain* (Paris, Les Belles Lettres, 1989, p. 264).

3   Paul Du Breuil, *Zarathoustra et la transfiguration du monde* (Paris, Payot, 1978, p. 211). Eudoxe of Cnides, a student of Plato, and before him Xanthos of Lydia, claimed that Zarathustra lived six centuries before the expedition of Xerxes (1082 BC).

from the East. According to Du Breuil, in the seventh century BC in Babylon, there were among the Medes a caste of priests who held on to pre-Zoroastrian Mazdaism. These wise men professed the Mazdaist cult that Zarathustra had rejected because of its idolatry. Some of them claimed to have the ability of changing one's life into a dream. Among the self-proclaimed wise men among the Medes, Persians and Babylonians there were also magicians who practised occult sciences, astrology, sorcery and had nothing in common with the followers of Zarathustra. Later, there were also Chaldean and Hellenized *magoi*. They all pretended to be followers of Zarathustra, but not all of them were trustworthy. The false attributions damaged the reputation of the 'good religion' and the word Magi acquired a bad reputation[4].

The thesis on the presence of a "founder of the sect of Magi" appeared in different countries, with even as many sects of Magi, which is why we need to turn to *the Gathas* for reliable information on the forming of communities that developed centuries earlier. The first small communities consisted of enlightened sages who informed others of the new vision of life. By bringing a message of hope they tried to appease their souls and improve their lives (31,19). The good news was spontaneously disseminated through other participants who passed it on to their collaborators. The latter regularly addressed the ones who were inclined to go astray (31,17).

In short, the three categories of community members outlined in the *Gathas* were constituted by supporting individuals who respected the tripartite motto; sympathisers who firstly, learnt about their potential, secondly, were motivated to give this practice a chance, and thirdly, relied on one another to mutually reinforce each other and like-minded persons. These categories aimed to spread a way of life that was to be discovered individually and consolidated through contact with each other. In other words, the community life reflected the importance of the number three, the holy number, usually assigned to Pythagoras.

In the beginning, this organic division seems to have been limited to the entourage of Zarathustra, although we find testimony in the *Gathas* of Zarathustra addressing outsiders: "When once you come within our brotherhood, you'll understand the merits of true life". And a warning

---

4 For more detailed information on the Median Magi and the Chaldean Magi, see Du Breuil (1978, 200 ff).

is expressed to those who persist in following untrueness: "Should you choose to leave the brotherhood, then grief and words of woe shall be your end" (53,7). On the whole, these verses spread the need to be able to rely on strong men and women, searchers of trueness, who detected those who repel wisdom (32,1). On co-operators (from community and family), who were concerned about individuals showing an arrogant and hostile mentality. Also, friends and allies, who spread the new way of thinking (33,4) and offered protection against defamation and slander.

Glad tidings

Zarathustra addressed himself to his companions and bore witness to what he had experienced. It was a testimony of the joy he felt when he opened his heart to the inner confidant. To be sensitive to an awakening light is a recurring feature in many religions. Light functions as a signal that announces better times. In Zoroastrian religion, the light symbolism is not so much a reference to faith or belief, but to the possible outcome of perseverance or patience in an engagement. It can denote the merit of one individual, although the welcoming of the light that shines on the path towards more trueness is not associated with the life of a recluse. The message of hope and progression in the process leading towards endless light is tied to a life shared with others, which again undergoes several transformations over time.

The glad tidings in the *Gathas* announce better times are ahead. Implicit in the message is that response-ability leads to a long life in service of infinite wisdom. Followers of Zarathustra were probably attracted by this verse: "Striving for light, himself shall see the light" (43,2). It encouraged them to open up to the two opposing tendencies, and to give priority to the regenerative tendency, to the detriment of the other one that immobilizes. The assumption that humans are the living theatre of opposing forces, torn from both sides, this confession alone apparently had a liberating effect on Zarathustra's companions and gave them a space to retreat from their worries. It turned out to be an adequate way to reply to the threatening darkness; one that offered an unexpected relief.

We cannot deny that experiences of relief are extremely important in alleviating distress. Relief reflects the state of finding assistance; the heart is literally lifted. A joyful and fortifying feeling of hope must be what

Zarathustra expressed in some of the first verses. His exceptional and thought-provoking ideas probably awakened his companions one by one to the joy that he himself had experienced. "Consult your wisdom" and "let each with his inner self commune" (53,3), Zarathustra urged. Discover which tendency should be given priority each day and which should be countered. The truer person tries to live in accordance with infinite wisdom (45,3), and in his acts and heart will reach endless light (45,5).

Needless to say, the well-known expression 'glad tidings' has been associated with the promise of eternal life in terms of an afterlife, but Zarathustra's 'good news' is not to be misunderstood. His focus on the importance of self-examination and fighting hypocrisy begins with the confrontation of one's own mechanisms of twisting the truth. To recognise the power of falsehood constitutes an incentive to take part on a daily basis in an evolution towards more trueness. Moreover, there is no promise of light pouring down on believers as a result of their faith and good deeds. To reach endless light, with reservations regarding the unknown, implies a lasting way of life that is not attainable on the spot. The meaning of reaching endless light is reflected in this verse concerning the truer person: "His wisdom (…) shall grow from day to day throughout a long-continued existence" (43,2).

The 'good news' Zarathustra tried to spread was not about receiving something, and is to be distinguished from the promise to 'receive eternal life' in the Christian sense. The difference between receiving eternal life and reaching endless light is yet to be found in the personal effort one is prepared to make during one's lifetime in the striving for light; in the effort that is required to resist falsehood and not give in to bending the truth. When we address our fears instead of looking away from them we may find they have an enlightening potential: things can become clearer when we succeed in reformulating or reorienting our thoughts. To reach endless light refers to the gradual process of reducing the paralysing power of anxieties; of experiencing a kind of bliss in resisting to old habits, which otherwise would not go away.

The symbolic meaning of glad tidings has crossed the continents, revealing the generosity of the light, its clarifying or heart-warming power that may actually work like a blessing. Let us not forget that among the descendants of the Magi there were the three wise men coming from the east to Bethlehem, bearing gifts to the new-born king, and setting off again on their journey[5]. To follow a star is more than a one-time experience, however powerful the experience may be. Endless light does imply so much a duration, but a condition that blurs the distinction not between this life and the so-called afterlife, but between life and non-life. This symbolic language is most powerful in conveying the meaning of the better times that are ahead. Many have repeated after Zarathustra: "The light will stream through all the lights" (31,7).

The light metaphor

A well-known legend tells us that Zarathustra made light visible. To make light visible is an original expression, a metaphor emphasising the importance of growing awareness. To become aware of something means to distinguish it among other things, to clarify it, or to cast light upon it. In hindsight, not the things that can be perceived are clarified, but that which speaks to our self-awareness, that what matters. The human eye is a receptor of light and the human body a capturer of light energy. Some will say that we are part of the light. All living beings are sensitive to light, and what is more, responsive to light. Human perception is very limited when it comes to evoking such existential experiences. So, sometimes symbols are more powerful in direct communication.

To strive for light, to reach eternal light, to speak to the light, are all expressions denoting what Zarathustra intuitively experienced as an illumination. Light, as opposed to darkness, thus became a parameter of awareness. Even in his day, Zarathustra observed that there is only a tiny light in those who despise or ignore trueness: "False ones shall for ages long reside in darkness (…) by their own selves, through their own deeds" (31,20). Many questions arose in him: how could he convince them not to remain in the darkest of places? Did they simply ignore the possibility of another life? Did his predecessors fail to teach them how to escape slavery? Would he himself be able to encourage them to develop their individual understanding?

Now, among the deceitful who find themselves in the darkness and regret, who are lost by their acts (31,20), he distinguished the men and

---

5   A.V. Williams Jackson declares: "It was the Magi—true followers of the ancient faith of Persia, those wise men from the East—that came bearing gold, frankincense, and myrrh to the babe at Bethlehem" (Matt. 2:1–2): https://en.wikisource.org/wiki/Avesta,_the_Bible_of_Zoroaster

women who display an openness for a better way of life. He discovered the enlightening potential of men and women who yearn for the light. Together with them he tried to unmask the bad leaders and fraudulent persons who abuse their power of speech to defend their inconsistencies. If nothing else, he made them realise that specious reasoning does not equal doing what is just; being intelligent or eloquent is not enough to promote justice. His intuition had told him that "the best life is that of who strives for light and shares it with others" (43,2).

Let us be clear that Zarathustra hoped his listeners who aspired for light would discover solidarity with others who also cared for the planet and its inhabitants. That they would feel encouraged to take action; that a first spark would be produced in them that would radiate the universal light passively present in each individual. Would they understand that corruption makes individuals abuse their power in order to defeat others and what's more, pass their own non-life unto others? Being fundamentally jealous of the good life right-minded persons lead, they organize conspiracies against them based on fear, scary demons and superstitions. What they cannot see is that in depriving themselves of a better life, they are also depriving others of what stimulates inner growth (43,15).

Through the light that gave him insight into how things are connected, Zarathustra discovered the hidden link between human intelligence and the intelligibility of the universe. This means that the lucidity which perceives the dynamism of the universe also makes the universe intelligible. He had a first awakening in the form of a bright light coming towards him, almost like a sunrise at daybreak. Suddenly, there was the impression that the light was speaking to him and that he could reply; that he even could address infinite wisdom and talk about his anxieties; that he could confide in it – an experience that is sometimes seen as mystical and special, but is in fact very real and profound. The whole experience inspired him with this reflection on the real disposition of man: "Dark is the mind of those that cling to false; but brightly shines the mind that follows trueness" (30,4).

Confidential friendship

Thus spoke Zarathustra to the light: "May I ever hold you in my mind as the first and also the last. As father of good thinking" (31,8). An alternative translation to 'the first and the last' proposes 'the beginning and the end'. This verse, one among others, seems to evoke a monotheistic vision, which also explains why Ahura Mazda was associated by the European translators with God. In English, the repetitive invocation "O Mazda" has been translated by "O Lord", in French "O Seigneur", in German "O Herr", in Italian "O Signore". In the present reading, I propose to defer the monotheist appropriation in order to better grasp the process of abstraction implied in the yearning for light.

Bearing in mind that the relationship to infinite wisdom has an anthropomorphic structure – humans relate to any object or subject in a human manner – Zarathustra distances himself from the anthropomorphic images of the gods, which can induce a lack of respect among the uneducated in matters of loving wisdom. In seeking to pay the greatest respect to the source of a hidden dynamics, ever evolving, inaccessible, he wished to avoid the pitfalls of blind devotional adoration and to establish a friendly relationship. On the one hand, through his insight into cosmic dynamism, Zarathustra arrived at the conclusion that through awareness humans are capable of connecting with wisdom. That is the meaning of the passage on turning to the light shining within oneself and to come in contact with "the light that streams through heavenly lights" (31,7). This is also why he continuously encouraged his friends to open their hearts and their minds, to see with the eyes of the heart; without pre-eminence of reason nor pre-eminence of the heart, but with their indispensable cooperation.

On the other hand, he called upon the relationship to enlightening wisdom "as between friends". Obviously, an amicable relationship with something as ungraspable and impersonal as endless light is not something any mortal can achieve, especially if it is a dynamic principle to which humans pay the greatest respect. With regard to infinite wisdom, nothing allows us to speak, in philosophical terms, of an absolute, metaphysical entity. Each living being is connected with life-giving light, but human awareness allows individuals to engage in a caring relationship with what gives them the energy to live. Although humans experience also a separation in the connection with a sovereign energy, they can become personally involved in the process. Zarathustra believed in the fostering of a confidential relationship, providing that the confidant in the dialogic monologue is treated as a friend – friendship can of course not be the subject of bargaining and neither can it be enforced – and that the implied personification does not develop into an over-familiar relationship.

We thus come to the finding that in addressing infinite wisdom, Zarathustra installed a relationship that is both personal and impersonal. In not reducing Mazda, infinite light, to a sovereign authority, the generosity of the amicable relationship is not compromised. If wisdom is without representation and shines without reserve, it holds an aspect of endless love. This way, the passage on 'the first and last', 'the beginning and the end', can be read as a quality label attributed to Mazda, infinite wisdom, as being both the initiation and the initiator of an ongoing process of good thinking and good work: "Mazda is father of good thinking (*vohu manah*) and his daughter is dedication to good work (*armaiti*)" (45,4). The family character of these expressions implies a caring and friendly relationship with the representatives of wisdom.

To assign the quality label to infinite wisdom of both initiation and initiator is based on the idea that confidential friendship with infinite wisdom appears to be the best guarantee for friendship on earth, not only between humans, but also with the other living beings. This is a first answer to readers interested in this rather unknown tradition and eager to know to whom Zarathustra addressed himself to; whom his reply was directed to. If they wish to know whether the confidant Zarathustra addresses is a God, the creator of the universe, I refer to the next section on Zoroastrian genesis. If they are interested in a growing relationship with infinite wisdom, my hypothesis is that 'the first and the last' does not exclusively denote a godhead that will survive all other gods. Not necessarily a superior God is being suggested, but rather a supreme wisdom, as the initiation of more wisdom. The father who gives birth to good thinking and good work is not just the best God, the wisest God, but a supreme wisdom, without equal, no one being able to imagine a more unbelievable wisdom, an ultimate wisdom.

Process of abstraction

The *Gathas* are an exceptional document that contain the seeds of the process of abstraction from a polytheist culture to the vision of a single cosmic wisdom. They hold an emancipatory dimension that translate the shift from animist adoration and devotion to admiration and dedication. Representations of the gods were rejected by Zarathustra as a hidden means of subjugating the people. The most venerable relationship to divine light, to infinite wisdom was perceived by him not in relation to an external representation, but through introspection. Also, there is no sign of a God of Light or a Sun-God, comparable to Aton in Egyptian culture[6]. Neither of a possessive god, who wishes to keep his people for himself, or a jealous god who destroys the other gods. As a matter of fact, the absence of a possessive god prevents the divinities of other religions from being eliminated.

Far from pursuing a new religion, Zarathustra tried to preserve the people from polytheistic degeneration, such as they were subjected to in earlier Mazdeism, animism and polytheism. By looking after the individual small flame – this is the element to bear in mind according to Zarathustra – each person takes care of the universal light. The unseen perspective was indeed not to feel subjugated by arbitrary laws and to fit into a structured universe, inciting the ones who felt addressed to flourish. Zarathustra advised people not to flee from what at first may seem unattractive, from the unknown, at least if this can be perceived as taking a glance at unexpected light. This reminds us of the metaphor of light that shines in the dark, a cryptic formula, typical of sacred mysteries (Egyptian, Chaldean, Orphic), accused by monotheist religions of being pagan and heretical. Coming from the occult, it was integrated into the official religions without ever having received any recognition.

What is important is how, in Yasna 44, a dynamic presentation of the universe is deployed. Contemplation of nature seems to be a guideline for life in what can be qualified as the Zoroastrian genesis. Theses verses, in the form of a series of interrogations, speak for themselves: "What being laid down paths for the sun and the stars? Who made the moon to sometimes wax and sometimes wane? And also: "What architect fashioned realms of light and realms of darkness? Who wisely planned for us both sleep and waking, rest and work? Who created dawn and day and night, to make us understand the orientation of life?". And again: "Who has separated the earth and the sky? Who keeps the waters and the plants in place? Who guides the winds and the dark clouds?" (44,4).

Apart from the emphasis on the typical philosophical attitude of amazement, these verses can be read as the worship to one God. To Zoroastrians, Ahura Mazda is the first monotheistic God, which was actually the case in the Achaemenid empire (550-330 BC), when Mazdeism was a state religion. The following inscription is most enlightening in this

---

6   Hélène Blavatsky, *Les Origines du rituel* (Paris, Prisme, 1973, p. 38).

respect: "A great God is Auramazda, who created the earth, who created the sky above, who created man, who created happiness for man"[7]. In an inscription in Persepolis, the king Xerxes declares: "And where the daevas were worshipped, me I have worshipped with devotion Auramazda and Arta". By the way, Greek and Latin authors also used the one-word name Ormazd. And they identified Zarathustra as "the son of Ormazd". Plato, for instance, did not speak of Zoroaster the Magus, but textually referred to "the son of Ormazd"[8].

To return to the *Gathas*, we note that Ahura Mazda clearly plays an important role and that the six representatives of wisdom (*amesha spenta*) remain in infinite symbiosis with him. Ahura Mazda is mentioned more than 400 times, sometimes in inverse order as Mazda Ahura, sometimes without Ahura, sometimes without Mazda. On two occasions, Ahura Mazda is referred to in the plural (30,9 and 31,4) and in one strophe he is flanked by "the lords of wisdom that are his" (45,6). If preference is given in the present publication to the translation 'infinite wisdom', this is due to the life-giving aspect: "You gave form to mother-earth, to the waters and the plants" (51,7). As to the argument that this is not a creation out of nothing, but a creation out of wisdom, we can only refer to the creative and regenerative intellect of infinite wisdom[9].

Should the reader award the monotheist qualification to Zoroastrianism, he or she will find an affirmation in this verse: "He who denies the *daevas* and their men" and "who reveals the path of life, O Mazda Ahura, becomes friend, brother, father" (45,11). It is clear that whoever pays tribute to Mazda will find a friend in Zarathustra and that a growing relationship must be consolidated, time and time again. Nevertheless, rather than to identify Zoroastrianism as the first monotheism, it is more accurate to talk about a henotheism on its way to becoming a monotheism. The expression 'henotheism' was coined by Friedrich Schelling, a young colleague of Hegel, and it was picked up in 1869 by Max Müller in his study on Vedism[10]. It designates the belief in a plurality of gods with an alternating

---

7   Marcello Meli, *Inni di Zarathushtra* (Milan, Mondadori, 1996, p. XXVIII).
8   *Alcibiades I*, 122 a.
9   Almut Hintze considers with Gherardo Gnoli that there is no question of an ex nihilo creation, for everything comes from the goodness of Ahura Mazda (2014, 243).
10   Müller clearly distinguished between henotheism or the veneration of multiple divinities and monotheism characterised by the refusal of plurality, but without necessarily excluding monolatry. Friedrich Max Müller, *Beiträge zur Vergleichenden*

predominance of one of them. Henotheism thus evokes the possibility of one specific god being better or superior to others, a hierarchic constellation that does not exclude the veneration of other divinities[11]. In which period monotheism was a fact cannot be determined with any degree of accuracy. So, if Zarathustra advises against polytheism – which by the way was restored after him – it is mainly because the *daevas* are deceitful, not solely because there are more than one.

Cult of fire

For Zarathustra, human consciousness awakens the desire to protect. The readiness to protect the beauty of the world is one manifestation of the effect of light and fire. Zoroastrian fire consecrations are both a way of protecting the fire and of receiving protection. It works in two directions, not of course in an instrumental, but in a reciprocally supportive way. In the fire temples, where Zoroastrians offer a piece of dry fragrant wood to the fire, respect is paid to the different degrees of fire. They engage in individual prayers and rely on their experiences of the sacred and secret knowledge in performing rituals together and apart. Fire reinforces universal sympathy whenever the personal experience seems to be taking part in the impersonal process. This works also at a distance, even unwittingly, and it is more than symbolic when it enhances the wish to protect the inner flame, to take care of the individual universal fire.

It is important to not equate Zoroastrians with admirers of fire. The Western propagation of their being 'fire worshippers' was actually an invention of monotheist religions to denigrate the despised pagans. If anything, the sacredness and purifying aspect of fire as a ritual practice has shown to be fundamental, considering the importance of the hearth-fire in Indo-Aryan customs, celebrated in the *Vedas* and the *Gathas*. Fire is a central element, an icon of light, warmth and energy. Most

---

Mythologie und Ethnologie (Band II, Leipzig, 1869). In English, I refer to his *Contributions to the science of mythology* (London, Vol 2, 1897). Interesting is Müller's reaction to Darwin's *Origin of Species* (1859), which suggests that a struggle for life also takes place on an existential level, as a process of natural selection on the basis of natural elimination of the less strong and less happy.
11   Müller also forged the notion 'kathenotheism' in order to render the chain or rotation of deities in the Vedas, one by one supreme, thus emphasising the dynamic character of the universe.

understandably, the presence of fire burning in houses and temples comes in the form of a real flame. But it also has a highly symbolic meaning, when the inner flame is considered to elevate to a higher degree of cosmic energy. Better informed outsiders will probably no longer call them 'fire worshippers'.

In the *Gathas*, a reference is made to "the men that gaze with clear eyes on earth and sun" (32,10). In Zoroastrian rituals, all types of heat energy in nature and the different degrees of sacred fire are celebrated. Inside information on the sacred fire rituals both in Iran and India, on purification and on the intermediary role played by the priests in the ritual consecration of the sacred fire is now within everyone's reach[12]. When existential fire, the fire of life, is considered in relation with being true, with the fire of trueness, fire rituals can be seen as fortifying and protecting processes. To visit the fire temple, the sacred house of fire, is an act that reinforces the individual who calls upon the fire of enlightenment in his quest to become a truer person or to be protected against deceit. It is a way of connecting with fire as a unifying force, as an element that inspires a primary, instinctive, intuitive custom with an indirect consolatory effect.

"Whom other than thy fire shall protect me?" (46,7), is a verse that conveys the beneficial effect of fire being consolidated. In fact, it is not only the real fire that brings relief, but also the opening up of one's heart to the possibility of being comforted, protected or relieved. Relief in ritual practice has an almost nutritive effect, like taking in food and using it for growth. Moreover, the fire ritual also involves the confrontation with one's own inconsistencies. The readiness to be tested reflects the resolve to expose oneself to the test of trueness. If we do not succeed in elevating our inner selves, we might set ourselves the objective of passing "the fiery test" (30,7). The test of fire is therefore an examination of one's motivations, a confrontation with the masks we put on, a trial by our inner supreme judge. It is intended to make our dedication grow, and to sort out the brave, true and strong, inspired by wisdom (43,10).

This is where the "test of fire" becomes a fundamental exercise in the Zoroastrian cult of fire. Put to this test are "both parties, true and false". The ordeal by fire "lays bare their inmost souls" (51,9). On several occasions,

---

12   See for instance the website of a Parsi priest: https://ramiyarkaranjia.com/6-qa-about-fire-fire-temples.

Zarathustra mentions the exposure to the blazing fire of wisdom. To expose oneself to the "blazing fire" (31,19) is a way of measuring the real state of mind, especially in the confrontation with doubt. To elevate the inner self is perceived by Zarathustra as a sort of test, especially if one does not "understand what true and lasting progress might imply" (32,7).

The plant metaphor

With hands uplifted, Zarathustra directed himself up to the light of aurora. Turning to the light, like a plant, he had a vision of an awakening spirit. He was marveled by the light that enlightens the world, by an illuminative source that itself remains invisible. Astonished by the capacity to look inside himself, to be enlightened by an internal eye, he bore witness to this illumination in the dark, of a spark igniting (43,1). Like a planted seed in the darkest of places bursting open and growing towards the sunlight, Zarathustra took part in a kind of self-regulation of nature. He praised the beauty of flowers blooming while following a foreseen path. To him, a seed is not what it is, if it cannot become fruit or if it cannot bloom into a pretty flower. The blossoming of the flower is not the purpose; it shows how nature drives itself towards completion.

For Zarathustra, the way of nature can be perceived by humans as an uplifting insight. All they need to do, is to observe the world of plants and animals and feel invited to participate in the universal sympathy. Indeed, in an unexplainable dynamism, the idea came to him of an inherent and effective solidarity between everything that exists. By carefully watching how the evolving universe develops in the tiniest of beings, humans can cooperate to improve the condition of all beings. In asking ourselves about the deeper meaning of blossoming together, of taking part in what is life-fulfilling, we probably need to learn more about the extremely ingenious system that makes all things obey to the laws of nature. For instance, we breathe in oxygen and exhale carbon dioxide, while plants do the opposite, each individual element following the good rule of nature. Zarathustra affirms his readiness to obey to the rule of life (44,8), always expressing his amazement: "Who made the son obey the father?" (44,7). And he confirms that he wishes to dedicate his whole self with all his strength (44,9), asking to be taught how to keep dedication in his heart (44,10).

In a projection of the plant metaphor to human life, humans should ingest what allows them to grow. My suggestion to compare the human condition with growing plants and trees helps us realise that humans are essentially dependent on natural resources. In the case of plants, with processes like photosynthesis, there is a conversion of light into energy to grow. Thanks to water and sunlight, plants are their own food source, and together with feeding other living beings, they also nourish the conditions of nourishing. This could offer some insight into what is twice beneficial for each person on an individual level and the community, as also for the environment. We are not just alive, but we aspire to the splendour of fulfilment. Everything that comes to life, in a singular way, contributes to the greater picture of what is life-giving.

Now, when the natural order of nature is disturbed, it is important that we try and set things right. This is evident in the *Gathas*, in the wish to protect both upright persons and mother earth against ill-thinking teachers, who are destructive of life, self-centred, and who poison earthly food. Zarathustra knew that mental growth goes hand in hand with environmental well-being. There is this important passage on mother earth: "She is indeed our refuge who brings soul-strength and life-renewed" (48,6). She must be protected, so that man, animals and plants are happy and fulfilled. "Joy-bringing mother earth" cannot be left to those who "think thoughts of selfish gain" (50,2).

So, the nourishment of life energy itself must be protected against those who pretend to do good deeds, but then take possession of people's goods" (32,11). Individuals who are unaware of the divine plan, who are "voluntarily deaf" (32,12), think of themselves as victorious, when really they become "victims, doomed to slavery" (32,15). Zarathustra never ceased to repeat that a better life awaits those who devote themselves to the nourishment of life itself, which is also beneficial for animals and plants, as he claimed. He insisted on the inherent potential of each being to attain fulfilment or completion; on the transformation of the desire for possession into a quest for more wisdom. His interlocutors were invited to participate in trueness through knowledge connected to what is actually taking place.

Zarathustra dared to decide on the future: "He who aspires to understand what real life is, will later understand it" (51,19). Perhaps we need to remind ourselves indeed that to try each day to make better choices is a good way of coming to terms with our own inconsistencies. That the reward of this effort lies in resisting old habits, in persevering and in continually attempting to overcome indolence. The final stanzas of the *Gathas* express the hope that in the first small communities there "will awaken the desire to teach humanity by its action, by its way of being" (51,19). Zarathustra relied on the capacity of growth, on the development of more illuminating thoughts for continued progress, which also implies that he was preoccupied with "those who have the burden of protection and those who need to be protected" (29,7).

Growth

The disruption of the natural order is a well-known problem in our present-day society. Growth and fertility are severely threatened. The fertility of the new generation for example has fallen and thousands of species are threatened by extinction. We have reversed natural processes and have modified them by genetic manipulation. We intentionally intervene in the natural development and neglect the strength of natural regeneration. Through intellectual cunning, we invert the means and the end. The deceitful effect is sorely visible: we look away from the results of our actions. We promote the improper use of natural resources and give free rein to instrumental and exploitative approaches. So can we still see growth as a metaphor of life?

Before all, a good environment in which one can engage to serve the fertility of the earth, is the highest reward humanity can aspire to (34,14), observed Zarathustra. Growth is more than a symbol when it is seen as a perpetual movement of secret inspiration. This must have been how a precarious kind of community building first came to life, based on the idea that self-esteem grows in accordance with honest work, with as guideline that whoever cultivates the earth improves justice. It is the best way to grow strong and face the "rotten mass of lies". Most premonitory are these exclamations: "When bloody tyrants, following untruth, rush in from every side, who'll stand erect and upright?" (48,11). "When shall the rotten mass of lies dissolve?" (48,10).

Zarathustra's proto-ecology is formulated in such a way that we can easily recognise the distorters "who disturb the scheme of life" (32,9). They bring confusion and "poison spiritual nourishment" (32,10); they "hinder all fulfilment here below" (32,11). What is remarkable is that he experienced the unattractive aspects of life as not being fundamentally negative. Instead of thinking in terms of black and white, he discerned different shades of light and darkness that enrich the human mind. He did not turn a blind eye to the dark and obscure elements in humans, as he himself had experienced doubt and fear. Again, his own experience made him encourage everyone to carefully discern what life teaches us in the readiness to renew our perspective with an open mind. When in doubt, he stated, we should examine our dedication by "the heart and head of each of us" (31,12).

This philosophy has been passed on based on different degrees of shining light breaking through as the elementary conditions for growth. In the cooperation of mental growth and making things grow, humans can grow strong and become co-workers of wisdom. Sometimes, rituals are performed to nurture this experience of good workings. To seek refuge in prayer and offerings brings consolation and helps to get through difficult times. In the midst of a profound and obscure uncertainty, a strengthening process can indeed take root. To express gratitude and thankful joy, to honour the water, the fire, the mountains, the wind can unmistakably be experienced as a kind of mental nourishment. It simply gives expression to the fact that not all good things can be ascribed to the merit of human beings. "Mazda has covered the earth with food for humankind" and in return, "it has nourished mankind since the dawn of life" (48,6), maintains Zarathustra. Which is why he underlines the human responsibility of protecting mother earth: "Let not bad rulers rule us (…) toiling for mother earth" (48,5).

With Zarathustra, we arrive at the conclusion that true inventive power comes from discerning different kinds of darkness. For instance, what seems unattractive at first sight may provide an invitation to shed a different light on it. A temporary dwelling in darkness is not necessarily negative inasmuch it can induce us to rephrase our words or rethink our actions. To patiently reside in darkness can be beneficial when one is prepared to consider it as an effective source of regenerative power. Positive symbolism can indeed in our individual lives function as an incentive to wade through dark times, to take initiatives and to let time do its work. Instead of prospecting bad times ahead, which may generate indifference or defeatism, individuals gain confidence when they start to communicate with the inner self "in order to benefit from intuition" (53,3). This is when Zarathustra makes us understand that no darkness is definitive, unless we are dealing with a sterile obscurity where nothing can grow, where the light barely penetrates (53,6), a state of non-life.

Part Two. Who? 73

Proto-ecology

The following lines express encouragement: everyone begins "to communicate with their inner strength". "Intuition must gain ground", so that "everyone gains confidence in clear understanding" (53,3). These elements of inner strength, of intuition and confidence are so characteristic of this arch-practice that depends on an ecological awareness. A form of proto-ecology is obvious in Zarathustra's reply to the scream of mother earth. This archetypical trait of humanity as a call for more peace and justice continues to reverberate for us even today, with the imposition of urgent matters regarding a liveable environment (see part V). There is a growing body of opinion that current ecological problems can only be seriously addressed if more humans are implied.

In the final *Gathas*, Zarathustra asks for more divine wisdom in the hope of sharing it with others, including those who "are deeper in confusion" (49,1). The best choice man can make is to stimulate those who "spread the message leading to perfection, who release it and teach it" (31,6). All along his difficult experience with false teachers, Zarathustra continued to share his liberating experience with his companions and believed it had a social, inter-subjective and beneficial dimension. The spreading and sharing was definitely a recurring element in his attempt to mobilise others by the radiance of energising light.

Now, if an ecology of wisdom is to be liberating, then it must combine good thinking with consistent practice. Zarathustra insisted on this point: "Integrate the proper understanding in your life" (53,5). Let us point out once again that the willingness to follow the tripartite motto only once in a while will not be enough to experience its beneficial effort. The motto needs to be put to practice and be constantly renewed and nourished, like watering plants. In Zoroastrian festivals, the four elements (earth, water, fire, wind or air) are powerfully symbolized and are kept free from defilement. Given the direct contact with fertility and abundance, agriculture has been one of the noblest of all activities in Zoroastrianism. Growing one's own food brings joy and happiness and working with plants and animals is one of the most delightful and gratifying activities there is.

Having himself experienced the energy that stems from perseverance, Zarathustra stated that "only hard and persistent work can lead to the understanding of your inner strength in order to use it for a better life"

(51,19). This work implies both the willingness to examine your conscience and to take up the challenge of a long-term commitment. No strength or change in human existence will come from outside alone. Each individual must decide for himself if he or she feels up to the hard work that lies ahead and will learn from experience how far it can be assimilated with participating in 'universal intelligence', in 'cosmic energy', and eventually in advancing towards what is called endless light.

This vision allows us to discern both a mental and an environmental ecology in the *Gathas* on which the evolution of humanity depends. The ecology of wisdom experienced as an enlightenment by Zarathustra was perceived as something that may actually "help our maids and men" (53,8). "So, let them strive with thought, and word and deed" (53,2), he urged. In projecting the nourishing chain onto humanity, the growing and the blossoming, it is the process towards completion, towards an ever-renewed completeness that is put forward. Of course, Zarathustra knew that to choose for hard and persistent work is not something that can be imposed. "Let each one choose" (53,2) is a clear incitement in this ecology of wisdom: use your intelligence, or even, dare to think for yourself. A sort of Delphic principle "know thyself" can be found in Zarathustra's hymns. Horatius's motto "to dare to know", in Latin *sapere aude*, was formulated more than three thousand years ago. Thinking for yourself demands a certain courage, particularly one of self-criticism. With the additional remark that he who thinks for himself will not necessarily be liked for his ideas.

Zoroastrianism

In this chapter, we have discovered some essential elements of the Zoroastrian tradition. First, the symbolism of light opposed to darkness. Second, the dynamic orientation towards the light by those who brave the darkness. Third, the importance of the individual approach, which can become a shared commitment when several individuals turn to the light. Fourth, the warmth stemming from a shared commitment is beneficial to the regenerative process on an individual and social level, and on an environmental level. Zoroastrians do not walk in the footsteps of Zarathustra, nor do they try to follow or copy him. Rather, they inspire each other to start walking using their own legs, along with fellow travelers, against destructive forces.

In the past, Zoroastrians restricted the sharing of wisdom to their own communities. They honoured their tradition and kept it as a well-guarded secret in order to protect it from falling prey to destructive forces. They never practised conversion and believed that if it were to flourish, the Zoroastrian way of life should be protected from non-Zoroastrians. Furthermore, unworthy goals and bad habits are best addressed at an early age. If not, they will stand in the way of the development of a trustworthy community life. Zoroastrians have in fact a holistic world view and believe a person's thoughts, words and actions have repercussions in the wider world. The best case scenario is that individuals act consistently and revitalise their participation in the ingenious plan of nature.

Of course, the willingness to observe the tripartite motto is not enough to be a Zoroastrian. Zoroastrians are the inheritors of an age-old rituality and rightly consider themselves as the guardians of an unbroken chain of practice that benefits all livings beings. Differently put, they presume that to maintain the tradition alive will ultimately lead to more happiness and fulfilment for all. In principle, the idea is that 'good tidings' are there for anyone who, through self-examination, also seeks better relations with others. Again, the tripartite motto can only have a good social impact when it is mutually shared. But in the confrontation with other religions, with leaders who try to impose their own views and are not inclined to take into consideration the importance of honesty and respect, the Zoroastrian communities have been forced to protect themselves.

The history of Zoroastrianism shows several periods of attacks, of forced conversion and persecution, of attempts to eradicate the religion, of exile and diaspora. The result of the persecutions is that the surviving communities relied only on each other, which has caused procreation problems. The prohibition of marriages with non-Zoroastrians was probably accelerated with the incursion of Arab Muslims from the 7th century onwards, and during the diaspora from Iran to India, especially in the 9th century. No one can contradict the fact that the communities have been most vulnerable to external forces, which might explain a turn to a self-proclaimed orthodoxy. More 'orthodox' members claim traditional customs should be strictly maintained, while more 'progressive' Zoroastrians wish to put an end to the prohibition of marriages within the community provoking fertility dysfunctions over the centuries. Today, the important issue of intermarriage with non-Zoroastrians and the numbers of Zoroastrians being in decline has enhanced the dilemma to overcome the biological obstacles.

Another important point is that Zoroastrianism underwent influences of Hebrew, Greek, Roman, Seleucid, Parthian, Sasanian, Chinese origin. The impact through the ages of these and later influences, under Hindu, Muslim and British rule, on the self-definition of Zoroastrians cannot be underestimated. Besides the external impact, there is the internal fragility with regard to self-perception. Throughout history, the diverging approaches of Western scholars has been the cause of disagreements with regard to the definition of Zoroastrian religion. Zoroastrian scholars, together with the clergy, obviously feel responsible for a cautious approach to a rich heritage. The result is the promotion of an essentialist approach, the wish for a Zoroastrian 'identity' that is able to overcome internal divisions, which are all but favourable in the context of current world politics. Of course, non-Zoroastrians can only offer an outsider's view, but it looks as though these last decennia the interest for Zoroastrian ethics has been on the increase worldwide. Whether this is due to a need for a proto-ecological approach or to a strong upsurge in the faith, there is a growing conviction that it would be a pity to allow the falling birthrates of Zoroastrians to determine the destiny of Zarathustra's thought.

Zoroastrian division

In our globalising world, we are more and more exposed to other cultures and religions. Despite the existence of interreligious platforms, we can also witness the movement toward segregation and isolation. All religions fear that secularisation will affect the continuation of traditions, or that the multicultural mingling of people with different backgrounds will cause uniformity. Many Zoroastrians today are reluctant to go along with a secularisation process, at the risk of the Zoroastrian tradition being dispersed. Nevertheless, a policy of action has entered the hearts of those who consider that there is a universal dimension to Zoroastrianism. Zoroastrians may be reluctant to share their beloved prophet with other peoples, but they also realise that to allow the religion to spread freely might be the only way for Zoroastrianism to survive.

To be addressed are major issues such as the safeguarding of rituals and whether this can be guaranteed only by those who have effectively been blessed by Ahura Mazda in the initiation rite. Who shall decide on which authority the worldwide dissemination should rely, on the clergy or on texts, on prescriptions, age-old habits and morals? The prospect of growing secularization causes Zoroastrians across the world indeed to struggle with fundamental questions regarding the survival of an immemorial tradition. Understandably, followers of the official religion continue to focus on the blood line. Even if this has caused incest and inbreeding in the past, the idea is still defended today that some basic conditions need to be fulfilled regarding filiation. In the past, Zoroastrian priests (*mobeds*, sometimes also called *dastur*) were sons of priests. When the religion was oppressed in Iran, fire temples were destroyed or transformed into mosques. From the late 19th century, some Iranian priests were trained in seminars in India, called *madressa*. The worldwide diaspora created the opportunity to form *mowbedyar* or assistants in other countries, offering a new perspective on Zoroastrian education[13].

A new issue in the debate has put the focus on who can be a *mobed*, through what kind of schooling and training (see Part IV). And what about women? So the question remains: should the official Avestan worship be passed on from father to son or at least take place in an environment of close symbiosis with Zoroastrian communities? Zoroastrian religious authorities who fear profanation or secularisation believe Ahura Mazda is the only authority who can intervene in the extinction of the 'race'. As I was told by some priests, the future is exclusively in the hands of individuals who put their lives in the hands of Ahura Mazda.

The division between Zoroastrians also concerns the issue of mobilising future generations. On a deeper level, this division reflects a concern for what is valued most. Either practicing the rituals and reciting the prayers and sacred texts, keeping alive ancestral practices, including that of following the bloodline, or understanding what constitutes a consistent way of life in order to progress towards perfection. Evidently, each individual is free to examine his or her motivation and decide which dimension should prevail. Without excluding the option that these dimensions can coexist and even that they can reinforce each other. In my opinion, the two approaches – practicing the religion and passing on the way of life to others – are not mutually exclusive. Is it too farfetched to suppose that people who feel stimulated by the Zoroastrian principles,

---

13   I wish to make reference here to *Fezana Journal* of the Federation of Zoroastrian Associations of North America, containing precious information on Zoroastrian communities throughout the world, Archeological findings, Interfaith, Seminars, Gatha Study Circle.

could implement them in their lives? Of course, this raises the question of para-Zoroastrianism (see Part IV).

A beautiful line in the *Yasna haptanhaiti* goes like this: "We honour the bifurcation of the paths and their reunion"[14]. To trust the course of events is fundamental when one considers that the disagreements between Zoroastrians are not insurmountable. The choice to practise the good religion is materialized by youngsters who agree to pass the famous *rites de passage*, denoting the passage from childhood to adulthood[15]. Newly inspired generations rely on more transparency and less authoritarian leadership, but also show concern for the continuation of the religion. They are eager to properly continue Zoroastrian initiation, the consecration of ritual offerings to the water or the collective recitation to accompany death ceremonies[16]. Maybe internal divisions can be reduced on the basis of this line on preservation and guardianship: "In order to achieve the ultimate goal of a long life in harmony with trueness [...], I will fulfil the guardianship as planned" (33,5-6). To live is to progress together until blossoming, while showing respect for what is given. Again, there is this quotation: "The best refuge is a land that renews life" (48, 6).

Universal dimension?

The universal dimension Zarathustra had in mind, as follows from the *Gathas*, was not that of an all-inclusive Zoroastrianism. It is quite obvious that Zoroastrianism cannot be extended to the whole of humanity and that

---

14   (I, 20), the final prayer of *yasna haptanhaiti* (hymns not included in the *Gathas*, but of the same idiom and period). For further study, see 'Perceptions of the Yasna Haptanhaiti' by Almut Hintze, in *Le Sort des Gathas et autres* études *iraniennes. In mémoriam Jacques Duchesne-Guillemin* (ed. Eric Pirart, Louvain-Paris, Peeters, 2013).
15   The Zoroastrian initiation rite is called *navjote*, a ceremony that can take place from the age of seven to fifteen. After the initiation, a white cotton shirt is worn under the clothing (*sudreh*) and it is tied around the waist over the shirt, by a cord (*kusti*).
16   Zoroastrians do not bury the deceased, nor do they incinerate them. The towers of silence (*dakhma*) are places where the corpses are ritually carried to and where they are abandoned to the vultures. This ancient practice has been replaced by the use of solar screens that accelerate the process of desiccation of the bodies, a solution that has been tested in Bombay by Homi Dhalla, the official representative of the religion. As President of the *World Zarathushti Cultural Foundation*, he wrote the script of the film 'Zarathushti Culture: A revival' (DVD, 1998).

Zoroastrian liturgy, which has evolved throughout the centuries, cannot be presented as a universal religion. Each religious appropriation that is addressed to all human beings should be treated with caution, especially when different religious leaders try to impose their own universal laws. Indeed, the universal reconciliation of all the peoples is put forward by religions that claim their principles can universally be accepted. So the universal value of religious doctrines is often confused with moral universalism, based on the meta-ethical position that some existential principles can be applied universally. A moral or ethical universalism values receptiveness to a wisdom that is more far-reaching than the boundaries of religious prescriptions.

Zarathustra defended the wisdom of being true to oneself and to others, in addressing "each one to bring down good thinking in your lives" (53,5). Because of its individual practicability, this love of wisdom can take root in many places. It requires local anchoring, a constant renewal and people who mutually inspire one another in openness. It can be compared, in Greek Antiquity, with what Stoicism meant by moral cosmopolitanism. The Stoics wished to extend love of self in an ever-widening circle, from self to family and friends, and to humanity as a whole[17]. Opposed to the antagonistic image of Greeks versus barbarians, the Stoic vision implemented the possibility of 'foreign' peoples gaining access to the idea of responsibility and free choice. They needed a universal language that could pass on this cosmopolite morality. To live in accordance with *logos*, with the laws of nature, meant that good governance cannot be restricted to one's fellow-citizens, that the boundaries between states and cultures are morally irrelevant.

Two remarks are in place. First of all, we need to distinguish between the universal dimension of religious ideas and political ideas. Religious universalists easily support the idea that all humans, and not merely fellow-citizens, come under the same standards, while political universalists, on the contrary, defend the idea that people of all nations can become fellow-citizens, citizens of the world. Today, universally applicable principles are easily criticised as a kind of cultural imperialism of the West, seen as

---

17 Later on, Christianity offered a concept that was an extension of Stoic cosmopolitanism. The Church Father Augustine – who was familiar with Zoroastrian ideas – gave this concept a twist in his presentation of the City of God. Citizenship in his view is limited to those who love God and the eternal Church. All others are limited to the earthly city, to the love of self and are bound to a temporal politics.

trying to expand its values. Even if the idea of a future world government is advanced, it will probably be perceived as the result of the Western universal declaration of human rights.

Secondly, rather than to regard 'universal' as a spatial term, we could focus on the temporal connotation. The expression 'universalisability' was suggested by Jacques Derrida to refer to a movement forward[18]. Coming from the East or the West, the North or the South, the universalisable dimension implied in the Zoroastrian way of life is more suitable when referring to a potential. Thanks to a growing conscience that virtually belongs to the whole of humanity, a mazdaphilic arch-practice involves everyone who revives nature's regenerative capacity, again and again. This practice depends on reliable individuals who are united in the name of love for all living beings[19]. In the eyes of Zarathustra, what is envisioned is not a society with cosmopolitan rights, not a polity functioning on an anonymous base, but the utopia of a loving brotherhood, virtually extendable to all, including the love for animals and plants.

The tone of the verses on the "union with *asha*" (49,8) confirms the necessity of community building (see next chapter). It is not enough that members individually "unite the higher self with *asha*" (49,9) and become involved in the process leading to the light. The best guarantee for this arch-practice to work on a larger scale is that of brothers and sisters who practise this way of life and inspire each other. They are "the saviours of our earth and follow the call of love" (48,12). In this verse, Zarathustra asks for the best blessing: "To all my companions also grant this gift" (49,8). The question of numbers, of how many are involved in the process, indeed

---

18 A *"universalisable* culture of singularities", 'Foi et savoir' in *La religion,* Jacques Derrida and Gianna Vattimo (Paris, Seuil, 1996, p. 28).

19 Probably because of universalistic optimism, hospitality without restrictions, the irrelevance of boundaries between nations and cultures, Jacques Derrida published a short essay addressed to "the cosmopolitans of all countries". This interesting expression conveys a cosmopolitan hospitality linked to the differentiation of countries. It translates the necessity of assigning limitations to unconditional hospitality. Derrida refers to Kant's cosmopolitan right to universal hospitality linked to two conditions – limited visiting rights, not permanent residence; private and public hospitality under the rule of law – and stresses that such a right is recognisable by the "traits of a secularised theological heritage". He mentions Saint-Paul who in (*Ephesians,* 2) opens the doors of the house of God to all citizens and co-citizens of the world. *Cosmopolites de tous les pays, encore un effort* (Paris, Galilée, 1997, p. 49ff).

plays a significant role in this proto-philosophy. It is virtually directed to each individual who wishes to contribute to a fairer society and not just to a minority of thinkers, so that no one is excluded in advance and that all men and women are virtually involved.

PART THREE
WHAT?

The birth of orientalism

According to the legend, Zarathustra was born laughing, which conveys the idea that from birth onwards he was never like anyone else. To be born laughing rather than crying speaks to our imagination[1]. New life is a joy, be it the birth of a child or the seasonal return of new life in spring. Beyond this literal meaning, there is also the underlying, implicit meaning of the inseparable nature of joy and pain. The change in the mother's experience, as pain turns into the joy of the first moment, is quite magical. Even more magical is the change of perspective when, for instance, a painful moment receives the positive impulse of a new start. Painful and joyful moments are part of the whole picture. They cannot be disjoined, though they do not occur simultaneously, and in a child the one easily converts into the other. Magic is the hidden force that drives the way we renew our look at the world. Zarathustra's 'existential magic' is about the possibility of new outlooks awakening in us, of being responsible for the free choices we make.

Let us now take a closer look at the basic elements of this oriental view on life by returning to the 18th century, the time when the West first got hold of the so-called wisdom of Zoroaster. Before the translation of the Avestan texts, 'knowledge' from the East was merely based on legends and rumours coming from the first travelers to Iran and India. The French merchant Jean Tavernier stayed in Isfahan and Kerman in 1647 and 1654. The Dutch Cornelis de Bruyn made illustrations during his three-month-stay in Iran

---

1   Osho (or Bhagwan Shree Rajneesh) popularised the Zoroastrian tradition. He was opposed to (Western) faith, because it is always blind. He declared: "If one has eyes, one does not have faith in light, one knows it". In 1987, he gave a series of conferences, published under the title *The Laughing Prophet: Talks on Friedrich Nietzsche's 'Thus spoke Zarathustra'* (Köln, Cologne and Boulder, 1987, p. 9).

in the 17th century. And Jean Chardin published his journey to Persia and India in 1711. These travelers testified of the faith in one supreme God, a God superior to other gods, and to what was perceived as a personification of the two principles of good and bad[2].

In what follows, we focus on the influence of European translations. In the first French translation of the Avestan corpus that Anquetil-Duperron published in 1771, no genetic distinction was made between the documents he succeeded to collect during his stay in India. The young French pioneer left in 1754 having joined the troops of the 'Compagnie des Indes'. At his return in 1762, he deposited 180 manuscripts at the Royal Library in Paris[3]. Assisted by Zoroastrian priests in Gujarat, he translated these texts and published them in 1771 under the title *Zend-Avesta* (Commentaries on the *Avesta*)[4]. The whole set also included a biography of Zoroaster, partly composed in New Persian.

What Anquetil-Duperron did not know was that the *Gathas*, written in an older language, had been incorporated in the *Avesta*. It was only in 1858, that the German orientalist Martin Haug discovered an important section written in an idiom dating back to the time of the *Vedas* and translated it into German[5]. Old Avestan or Gathic, close to Vedic Sanskrit, is a dead language. Like Sanskrit, an Old Indic language it is related to, it is no longer used as an everyday spoken language. Only the section of older hymns, called the *Gathas*, are ascribed to Zarathustra, although researchers like Almut Hintze have recently expressed serious reservations on ascribing the *Gathas* to one author only. Hintze suggests that the chants could be the work of generations of priests who compiled the message[6].

---

2 Kellens, 'L'Avesta, Zoroastre et les sources des religions indoiraniennes', www.clio.fr, 2004. Worthy of mention is also the survey of the opinions of Greek and Roman writers on ancient Persia by Barnabé Brisson (1590).
3 The publication by Abraham Hyacinthe Anquetil-Duperron, *Le Zend-Avesta, ouvrage de Zoroastre*, was controversial. He was accused by Diderot of having invented everything, and the imprecisions he found in the work of Thomas Hyde resulted in quarrels with the English orientalist William Jones.
4 Pierre Lecoq published a recent edition in French, *Les livres de l'Avesta. Les textes sacrés des Zoroastriens* (Paris, Cerf, 2016)
5 In 1854, having been awarded a PhD on Zarathustra, Martin Haug became an unremunerated university professor. From 1859 to 1866, he was a professor of Sanskrit in the Indian city of Poona. His translation of the *Gathas* was published in Leibniz in two volumes (1858-1860).
6 Almut Hintze, *Change and Continuity in the Zoroastrian Tradition* (London, Soas University of London, 2013).

Over more than one century, a mixture of later Avestan texts were indistinctly attributed to Zarathustra. Till the end of the eighteenth century, the 'expertise' on the Persian religion was based on the totality of sacred texts, commentaries on liturgies, ritual prescriptions of worship, which were altogether founded on a dualistic ethics. When Martin Haug published the *Gathas* and revealed that they were to be distinguished from the other Avestan texts, he underlined the absence of a dualistic ethics and of religious prescriptions. Since that time, the distinction between the *Avesta* and the *Gathas*, has been the cause of division between Zoroastrians and between specialists of oriental studies. Some Zoroastrians still rely on the liturgical use of all Avestan texts while others particularly value the small section of hymns, the 17 'chapters' of the Gathas as being more 'authentic', and as being the oldest verses dating back to the period of Zarathustra.

Interpreting the Gathas

On a visit to Iran or India today, travelers will probably come into contact with Zoroastrian culture, with Zoroastrians who are Zartoshti (in Iran) or, in India, *Irani* or *Parsi*. The different communities and individual followers of the religion share a number of rituals, such as the initiation rite (*navjote*) and the new year rite (*nov ruz*). These are mostly based on Avestan texts, composed through the ages, containing liturgical ritual and hymns of worship. According to Eric Pirart, the liturgical use of Avestan texts by Iranian or Parsi Zoroastrians today is based on a collection of later texts, including the Pahlavi books, among which the *Denkard*, a book of annotations dating back to the tenth century[7]. The Zoroastrian tradition has undergone many changes over time, which of course reflects its dynamic potential of being able to adapt to a context.

Now, to readers who may be eager to read the *Gathas*, I would like to address the following word of caution. It is important to bear in mind that each translation implies an interpretation. According to the culture or religion of the translators, different linguistic versions were generated that best corresponded to their own ideas and impressions. Because of the numerous and divergent translations of the *Gathas*, it is advisable not to limit oneself to one single version. With regard to English, there are several

---

7   Eric Pirart, *Les adorables de Zoroastre. Textes avestiques traduits et présentés par Eric Pirart* (Paris, Max Milo, 2010).

reliable translations, originating mainly from India, England and America. Most readers will probably tend to select a version in their own mother tongue, but my experience tells me that it is better to read at least two versions of the *Gathas* and preferably in two different languages[8].

Once we have dismissed the idea of the 'original' or 'authentic' thoughts of Zarathustra, we understand that no reception can be considered exclusive, and that we have to move to a metalinguistic scale in order to understand each other. This is evident from the fact that in international research, scholars will often refer to their own most trustworthy translators, who then become personal authorities. Among the international scholars, a multilingual approach is slowly filtering down to the readers, who come across interesting passages and discover contrasts with their own way of thinking. Maybe, they will feel inspired to integrate specific elements in their own way of life. Knowing that our mother tongue plays a significant role, it is always recommended to take into account an additional margin when transposing new ideas into our life.

Another consideration is that several underlying concepts are not explicitly mentioned in the *Gathas*. 'Responsibility' for example is obviously not a word used in the hymns, but its importance clearly appears through close reading and through the transposition into our own personal experience of the thoughts that are expressed and from their integration into our own lives. So, it is up to interpreters with an active sense of reception to implicitly grasp what is conveyed by the term 'responsibility'. As Walter Benjamin clearly stated, translation is not merely a matter of repetition; it is a generative act. On the one hand, active reception involves the risk of freely adjusting the text to one's own conception. A loss of authenticity is noted in the transposition to the personal approach. On the other hand, passive reception, based on what is learned by heart, borne by repetitive sounds, is an attempt to come as close as possible to the most fitting enunciation, breathing and immersion, with a charm that is not to be underestimated. There is no reason to reject either of these two approaches, but anyone who wishes to really understand these hymns will need to become acquainted with an unfamiliar language in the first place. Only then will it be possible, through repetitive experiences, to discover the extent to which they may resonate on a personal level.

---

8   My study is mainly based on the translations by Taraporewalla (1979), Dina McIntyre (https://gathasofzarathushtra.com), Marcello Meli (1969), Khosro Khazai (2011) and Martin Haug (1858).

New terminology

Referring back to the *Gathas*, there is the most interesting passage on what I have translated as two tendencies: "The truer one takes the initiative and addresses the other: among us, from the beginning, neither the thoughts nor the speech, nor beliefs or actions agree. Neither we nor our souls are in harmony" (45,2). In taking a closer look at the terminology, there is the mention of two *mainyus*: *spenta mainyu* and *angra mainyu* (45,2). In English, *mainyu* can easily be translated as *mind*, thus respectively *good mind* as opposed to *angry mind*. *Angra* is similar to 'angry', destructive, a meaning also found in the German expression *das Gute* and *das Böse*. In more recent English publications of the *Gathas*, translators opt for 'mentality' which is closer to *mens* in Latin[9]. The two minds refer to the two opposed mentalities, constantly at work in "in each thought and word and deed" (30,4).

'Mind' and 'mentality' are preferable to *esprit*, the translation of *mainyu* in the initial French edition by Anquetil-Duperron. The existence of two 'spirits', together with the evocation of a 'good spirit' opposed to an 'evil spirit', has caused an incorrect connotation, even an assimilation with demons (probably because of the demonised *daeva*). *Spenta mainyu* has in some interpretations even been identified as the Holy Spirit, probably because of this passage on Mazda as the "father of *spenta mainyu*" (47,3). This way, *spenta mainyu* was the Holy Spirit of the God Ahura Mazda[10]. While Ahura Mazda exerts the powers to further the good creation, he is in eternal combat with Satan, with the figure of the devil, Ahriman, a contraction of *angra mainyu*.

The two 'spirits' were thus welcomed in the West not as two opposite mentalities, but as autonomous entities, in a Manichean way: God and his rival govern over two cosmic powers, good and evil, as two autonomous masters, each with a reign revealed in the afterlife, called paradise or hell.

---

9   The Indo-European word *man* or 'thought' is an equivalent of *mens* in Latin. It was Kersee Kabraji who emphasised the use of 'mentality' in his work. See *Rationalism in Zoroastrianism* (Partridge, India, 2015). He defended the ideas of M.N. Dhalla, who in his *Zoroastrian Theology* (1914) disapproved of obsolete rituals and encouraged both rational study and spiritual development.
10 The first translation of *spenta* was 'holy', which was replaced by Almut Hintze by 'life-producing'. 'A Zoroastrian Liturgy. The Worship in Seven Chapters', Wiesbaden, *Iranica* 12, 2007.

In liberating the *Gathas* from such presentation, the more fundamental knowledge can rise to the surface. When one is arbitrarily submitted to external forces and attributes the events to arbitrary spirits, this does not induce human reflectiveness; it does not establish the presumption of responsibility. Instead of assuming responsibility, either the protected individual feels privileged and rewarded by good spirits or the pursued by demons claims innocence or takes refuge in the position of the victim.

This was how in the reception of Avestan concepts, all of the attention went to imploring the protection of good spirits in order to be safeguarded from bad spirits. This clumsy association with the descent on man of divine grace has reinforced the impression that one can chase the evil spirit in terms of rejecting the temptation of evil. Whereas *mainyu* refers to the mental world with its two opposite mentalities, this different meaning has indeed been conveyed and the knowledge regarding the two 'minds' was unwillingly transformed into a conception of 'good and evil'. Now, as soon as something is qualified in terms of good or bad, we introduce these supposed static entities into the frame of reflection. For this reason, I believe we need another frame of thought than that of good and evil, as the next chapter shows.

Whether it is advisable to propose new translations like the one suggested in this book is a matter for discussion. To bring forward the implicit movement in what I consider first and foremost as mobilising tendencies, seems to me more in line with the dynamic kind of thinking I derive from the *Gathas*. Tendencies are mental movements towards which we are directed in word, thought and action. The tendency to trueness and the tendency to untrueness correspond with the actual mental work. So, we can re-read the respective passages and find out how the use of 'tendency' suggests a movement, while bearing in mind that even the translation in terms of the two opposed tendencies does not prevent their assimilation with a good or bad tendency. In which case the bad tendency refers to the inclination of self-deception, the misleading of others in the name of self-interest, while the good tendency implies the resistance to untrueness by a good understanding of the freedom of choice. Be this as it may, the accent is on the underlying dynamic tone in Gathic expressions like "the truer one", who tries to live in accordance with infinite wisdom and who furthers the good creation. Important is to note the degrees in what we tend towards and the direction implied, towards more trueness or fading further away from it.

Good and evil?

Let us reconsider the elements we dwelt on in Part One; the opposite tendencies in the human mind and the primordial choice. Yasna 30 mentions the two tendencies, while the confrontation between *spenta mainyu* and *angra mainyu* is explained in Yasna 45. Zarathustra conceives both tendencies as dynamic and interdependent movements, with however an essential difference. Whereas the latter tendency is only designed to eliminate its opposite, the tendency towards more trueness allows us to address this unbalanced position. It is more autonomous since it draws its energy from *asha*, from the self-regulating principle of trueness. The individual who takes the path of more trueness and tries to follow the more truthful course of things will discover also in others the beneficial effects of the self-regulating process.

We are told that the path taken by the individual who resists dishonest acts and chooses not to distort his actions will turn out to be beneficial for others. Indeed, continuing on the path to more trueness involves a mutual concern for the progression towards a true way of being (30,5), which I personally wish to call regenerative. The *ashavan*, the follower of *asha*, is truer or better than he who follows deceit, *dregvant*, the deceiver, liar or cheater. We should give due credit to Dina McIntyre for gearing us towards a new approach, for highlighting the gradations on a scale from best to worst. McIntyre proposes alternative categories to qualify more precisely what is formulated in the *Gathas* in terms of 'the truth' or 'the lie'. She tries to solve the problem of entities like good and evil by translating the word *spenta* as 'beneficial'.

I refer to McIntyre's website with the most recent translations of the *Gathas*, pointing out that *spenta mainyu* appears along with the superlative *mainyu spenishto*. McIntyre's suggestion to indicate gradations in our actions is an implicit way to underline the mobility of the mind. It is important to operate in life according to a degree of progression, to what is best (*vahishta*)[11]. We try to find out in a particular context which actions are more or less beneficial, rather than to formulate a definition of what is good

---

11 I fully subscribe to the progressive movement of the evolution towards eternal light. If all creation evolves towards fullness, towards perfection, the evolutionary development is to be highlighted. The way someone lives his life can indicate in how far they are interested in goodness.

or bad in a moralising tradition. This new approach, as we will see further, corresponds to a slow letting go of the 18th and 19th century interpretation of the *Gathas*, which implies a distancing from the Latinisation of the Indo-European language, and a drawing closer to what Nietzsche understood by going beyond good and evil.

This disconnection of the *Gathas* from the concepts of good and evil yields an additional advantage. It liberates Zarathustra's hymns from the Manichean approach that was imposed over the centuries and generated the dualism of good and evil governed by two cosmic powers. Not only the Iranian prophet Mani maintained the opposition of two autonomous masters, the good god and the evil devil fighting to rule the world, he also introduced the theological problem of the origin of evil (see Part IV). By whom was the evil spirit created, by God or by Satan? How was a good God, creator of the universe, able to create the devil? If God is the creator of all, then has he created both good and evil? An external force as powerful as the omnipotent God must have been the origin of evil. Also, if both sovereigns have a reign, called paradise or hell, places where souls will go after death, then humanity is divided into two categories of good people going to the heavenly heaven and bad people to terrifying hell.

While the Zoroastrian concepts of 'heaven' and 'hell' refer to the existential state during life on earth, the images of paradise and hell in the afterlife have been most influential on the notion that there is time to reconsider the way of life that we chose for ourselves[12]. At least as influential as the garden of Eden, the beautiful place Adam and Eve were chased from when they lost their innocence. In the Christian scholastic tradition, paradise on earth cannot be attained, because of the corruption of human nature. This conception was most common from the time of Augustine and it was contradicted by Dante, who suggested the possibility of paradise in a Zoroastrian way, the potential reaching of justice and bliss, thanks to the desire to gain perfection in this life. It took many centuries to liberate people from the fearful representations transmitted through the ages, from

---

12 Dina McIntyre mentions that the idea of punishments in afterlife first appears in Pahlavi texts and that "all Pahlavi texts were written two or more centuries after the Arab invasion". She does not exclude the introduction of "a punitive fiery hell of torment in the afterlife described in the Quran" in later Zoroastrianism. She suggests that after the fall of the Achaemenid kings and following the Arab invasion, the Zoroastrian religious establishment lost its authority "and resorted to threats of punishments in the afterlife to protect their income generating rituals".

the idea of guilt and punishment because of carnal transgressions. Besides, this liberation continues to be essential in the connection of knowledge and beckoning happiness.

The twinning

Throughout the *Gathas*, Zarathustra presents the twinning of *spenta mainyu* and *angra mainyu* as two principles that contradict each other. They are permanently at war and often seem irreconcilable. Unlike the Buddhist response to the awareness of discord for example – to go beyond the conscious act to find a basic peace of mind –, Zarathustra sees the internal conflict as an instrument of self-understanding. The unconscious bearer of the two tendencies ignores the fact that the two opposing tendencies can take possession of a person if they are not rightly addressed. Refusing to recognise the two tendencies in oneself is to fail to understand that prioritising one of them leads to a truer way of being. Conversely, the conscious bearer of the two tendencies understands that when the wrongdoer in himself does not subscribe to the importance of the tripartite motto, he "does the worst" (30.5). Still, if he is eager to advance in life, he reminds himself of the two tendencies which "do not agree in thought, word and action" (30,3). He faces the internal struggle and does not give up. He does not become indifferent, and perseveres in the daily fight against the counter-productive tendency, thanks to the tripartite motto. This way, he acknowledges his personal potential and he contributes to the progress of humanity.

With regard to the genesis of the two tendencies, and because he cannot tell which of the two came first, Zarathustra uses the image of twins: "At the beginning, there were two tendencies, which proved to be cooperating twins" (30, 3). The idea of a double offspring producing two elements at the same time, may sound quite paradoxical, but we recognise this in many civilisations. It is a recurring phenomenon in so-called archaic civilisations to make use of the dyadology or the original coupling, most often of a male and a female god. They reflect the enigma of genesis and are based on a biological interpretation, which is also the case in Zurvanism, based on a similar, Gathic vision of an archaic twinning. In Zurvanism, the twins were understood as two soulmates who fight for domination and demand the authority of a father. To solve the question, the Zurvanists proclaimed the authority of the god Zurvan, the god of time, who reserved or promised the authority to the firstborn.

From a logical stance, it is not easy to imagine how two opposing elements can simultaneously come from the same source. All explanations related to a genesis include this enigmatic element, sometimes a dogma that cannot be refuted. What is interesting to notice in the dualistic view of Manichaeism is the coexistence of light and darkness at the beginning of time. According to Mani, the light was invaded by darkness, which was originally separated from it. Darkness prepared an assault on the light and gave rise to the creation of the world. The dualism engendered through Manicheism led to the conclusion that the material world is a kingdom of darkness and to be depreciated. The luminous good world was associated with spiritual life and darkness with corporeal life.

This is the reason why I cannot insist enough on the necessity of liberating Zoroastrianism from Manichean interpretations. It is important not to confuse it with the body and soul dualism, with its associated ascetic lifestyle leading to paradise after death. In order to mark the extraordinary existential dimension of the Gathic chants, it seems to me important to specify that not God and the devil reside inside us, nor two spirits, but two tendencies. Zarathustra's concern was exactly to free people from blind faith or false promises, from distorted and frightening world views. Obviously, we cannot erase the representations that have been widely disseminated and have been accumulated over the course of history. We cannot unravel the many layers of interpretation, but we can refer back to the *Gathas* and to Zarathustra's dynamic vision of life in a less representational way.

The argument is that we can try to live in tune with the existential dimension of these verses and reintroduce them in our daily lives, and at the same time respect the enigmatic side of these sacred texts, which without our intervention will remain dead and without meaning. For the record, a concept like that of the original twinning may also enable us to put in perspective the topological destination of heaven and hell, usually associated with the final outcome of the kind of life we have lived. There is no reason to be blocked by the suggestion of an original twinning, by two tendencies in humans that do "not agree in thought, word and action". This presentation is not less enigmatic than mythical stories on the origin of good and evil in the world. But it surely has not given life to timeless rules, laws and prohibitions, suggesting without explanation that specific things are absolutely forbidden in the eyes of God.

Part Three. What? 93

Two abodes

Zarathustra suspected that offerings performed as a form of bartering encourage a shopkeeper mentality, like striking a deal with divinities to secure favourable treatment in return. What he wanted was to put an end to the mentality of exchanging, of giving in order to receive, which is no more than a ploy designed by a cunning mind. To lower oneself to bartering cannot possibly be the right way to approach infinite wisdom; it even shows lack of respect. Still, the alignment of Gathic texts with Judeo-Christian ideas has generated many speculations on the two abodes mentioned in Yasna 51. Up till today, the expressions heaven and hell are conceived as places where souls will go after death following an exemplary life as opposed to a so-called sinful life. It draws the attention away from what I consider a precious tradition, and I find this regrettable. The dynamic vision of two opposite elements that function as verifying parameters in constant interaction with the surroundings is meant to make humans discover the true nature of a sovereign cosmic order. Their struggle to get the upper hand is not arbitrary, but entwined with the self-regulative principle called *asha* (see further).

What is called 'heaven' or 'paradise', derived from Young Avestan *pairidaeza*, 'enclosure', is not the appropriate translation of the 'best of abodes' (*demana garo*) or the 'house of song' (51,15). Actually, the association of paradise as an ideal place, where age and pain do not exist and good food is offered each day, was invented at a later stage and it is similar to the Garden of Eden as a mythical, oriental garden. Adam and Eve where chased from paradise, from the Garden of Eden, as their disobedience to God was not to remain without consequence. At least, this is the usual interpretation of the transition from innocence to guilt, also called the fall of man or the original sin, to which we may add another interpretation. Eden was a garden with two trees, and eating from the tree of life was no problem. But Adam and Eve ate from the tree of knowledge, meaning that they were suddenly aware of what was right and wrong[13]. In fact, the birth of conscious awareness, of the awareness of free choice was not about becoming sinful, but about initiating the process towards more

---

13 Adam and Eve by eating of the Tree of knowledge were suddenly aware of what was right and wrong, meaning they no longer were guardians of the Tree of Life, of eternal life. Not so much the longing for the initial state, called paradise and the regaining of innocence, is to be highlighted, but the knowledge and awareness of the process leading to the victory of light over darkness.

trueness. Only by acquiring the knowledge of the two kinds of existence can humans reach enlightened life and choose life over non-life.

In Greek accounts of the ancient Persians, the term 'paradeisos' referred to a garden where trees grow, where good things germinate and flourish, possibly where water flows freely and flowers bloom. The Avestan paradisiacal enclosed area is not the place where humans wish to return, a place where all suffering ends. It is not even a place in heaven, no more than burning hell is a place in the underworld. The two abodes refer to the condition of life and non-life on earth, both leaving the option of progressing towards the light. As a rule, the invention of the two abodes was an efficient way of making people understand that their actions will not remain without consequence, that human actions will not be forgotten, and that there is a future. To "gain dedication and to inherit all that the earth confers" (46,19) is without any doubt a better condition for each individual.

So, if the heavenly reward of endless light must have been the most attractive option, the prospect of dwelling in the "place of bad existence" was certainly a terrifying weapon. In the past, the risk of burning in hell was obviously frightening and it functioned as a strong incentive to change one's life. The expression "to harvest what you sow" comes close to a hymn like: "The false ones through false teachings, evil deeds, who drag the world into destruction, at last shall dwell in the abode of deceit (*drujo demana*)" (51,14). This appears to refer to a final position, when no time is left to change course, and I read it as a warning, not only for the persons involved, but also for their surroundings. To be led into the abode of deceit, sounds like an imprisonment in darkness, which may be the temporary and necessary condition for light to emerge.

When the two abodes are approached as a one-time option, they exclude the experience of remorse, repentance or regret, and what is more, of the possibility of changing or adjusting one's course. Scholars of Zoroastrianism have different opinions as to whether the abode of deceit refers to a hell without limitation. Here again, different perspectives were generated in later times such as being released from hell after a period of time, which reflects the Christian purgatory or limbo. Only verse 46,11 of the *Gathas* mentions "the place of bad existence", reflecting the fear of a life-long imprisonment in darkness.

The two perspectives of heaven and hell, when they fall in the hands of the power-hungry who expect blind obedience, function as false rewards or as threatening weapons. They become instruments of massive control and lose their beneficial working. Which is why I fall back on the aforementioned Yasna 51, on the pledge Zarathustra made to the brotherhood, to the followers of trueness: "Let each one listen to good thoughts in heart" (49,7). From my perspective, as I explain in the section on 'final judgement', to listen to good thoughts in heart takes time. A less categorical reading includes a degree of progression, different steps or gradations of advancing. It is based on movements of progression and regression, on the dynamic view of life implied in the *Gathas*. For now, let us say that the 'best abode' is that of people who time after time feel less inclined to deceive others, and the 'worst abode' is that of people who will not refrain from doing so.

Weigh bridge

The concept of a 'weigh bridge' is advanced by Zarathustra to emphasise the moment of evaluation, when we look in the mirror and become our own ultimate judge. Introspection is an instrument of moderation that helps us to abstain from judging others and to first look at ourselves (44, 13 and 44, 15). We know how often we are wrong and how often our bad habits outweigh our good efforts. So our deeds are weighed over and over again, until the time comes that we understand the benefits of this exercise, both for ourselves and for others. If more individuals experience the beneficial outcome of this worldview – according to this line of reasoning –, a prosperous future awaits us in a world advancing towards constant renovation.

Yasna 51 mentions the idea of a crossing place, called *chinvat peretum*, a symbolic bridge or passage we all walk across (51,13). Rather than the idea of a judge who punishes or rewards by sending the souls to hell or to paradise, there is this mention of a point of no return, a symbolic bridge or passage we cross. No doubt this bridge of judgement is associated with the time of our death, but it does not exclude the anticipated evaluation of our actions, as I suggest in this chapter. In any case, for Zoroastrians, the crossing of the bridge in the death ritual takes place on the morning of the fourth day after three days of prayer, of accompanying the *fravashi* (the highest principle) of the departed[14]. Predominating is the *fravashi* of the deceased, an eternal principle existing in all living beings, even plants. During three days, mourning and weeping are warded off, so that the transition towards the bridge may take place in the loving remembrance of the deceased[15].

The perspective of passing a point of no return might on a regular basis function as a stimulus not to let powerlessness or indifference get the upper hand. The moment we become our own judge in discrete relationship with infinite wisdom is obviously only part of the confrontation. It is a one-way consultation of a higher wisdom, including the possibility that our inconsistencies may outweigh our part of integrity. Now, the imagined mental transition towards the moment we reach our 'final breath' requires an openness to what we cannot even visualise. Important is the readiness to be exposed to the 'burning fire' as is clearly mentioned in Yasna 51.

Apart from the fact that an anticipated evaluation of our actions may have a liberating effect, that we resurrect from our non-life and enter into the best of abodes, the idea is raised that everyone will be exposed to the 'burning fire' and will be judged according to one's acts (51,9). The weigh bridge can be interpreted as the place where punishments or rewards are being enacted, but it can also be seen as an invitation to consider the great event of choice, referring to the doubt inherent in self-examination whether we are on the right path. It presents itself as a point of no return, as an absolute point in time. It functions as a signal for the individual who wishes to "be guided towards the light" (50,5). But not for the wrongdoer, as Zarathustra observes. The deceiver has a distorted image of the path towards trueness. He darkens his conscience by his own words and by his misleading deeds, Zarathustra affirms. "The false one has a crooked picture of the straight path, on judgement-bridge he will be taxed (...) through his own actions and his tongue untrue" (51,13).

---

14 There is a similarity with the concept of purgatory, an intermediate state after physical death, for those who have been both bad and good, who find themselves in a waiting period. Purgatorial fire is purifying, unlike the punitive fire of hell.

15 It is interesting to note that all deceased Zoroastrians are equally treated and that no monuments to the dead are being erected. Taraporewalla observes that the greatest monument to the dead is the mention of the eternal principle of great departed Zoroastrians at death anniversaries, as "the loving remembrance of their fellow men whom they had served" (1979, p. 63).

Of great importance is what is said about assuming one's responsibility: "On the bridge of estimation, he is blamed by his own soul and he goes astray from the true path" (51,13). In other words, even though the confidant inside him tried to make him understand that he will be blamed, still he chose to neglect this inner wisdom. Something inside him, the negative tendency, ultimately won and took over, probably crushing his self-esteem. This is what Zarathustra tried to prevent. He wished he could "save erring souls" (49,1). Till the very last second, he maintained, we long to "be guided towards the light" (50,5). We have longed for the "luminous pathway to happiness in the spiritual and corporeal life" and hope we will finally attain it (43,3).

In a more abstract meaning, the passage of the bridge can thus be seen as an invitation to assess one's actions and to imagine a final point in time when it will no longer be possible to conceal ourselves. To imagine the passage ahead reminds the wrongdoer of what he already knew, but has failed to implement; the daily choice is his. This reminds us of the Chinese wisdom in Confucius who recommended to live one's life as if it mattered for eternity, or Lao Tse, for whom heaven and earth were eternal, because they do not seek themselves (book I, 7). The intimate confrontation with the confidant, perceived in a positive and stimulating mindset, is not directed towards the goal of having little reason to blame oneself. Rather, when on 'judgement day' so to speak, the deceiver continues to find excuses, he will not have known the beneficial effects of a liberated existence.

Final judgement?

Among the scholars of Zoroastrianism, there is no consensus on the meaning of the weigh bridge and the fiery test (see Part II). The idea of a final judgement has often been interpreted in a Judeo-Christian manner as a final trial, even a sorting on judgement day with God as sovereign judge. As a matter of fact, the crossing of the bridge has been assimilated with a supreme judgement, a final trial in which the soul is evaluated by Ahura Mazda. On judgement day, God is the sovereign judge who decides whether we are among the chosen ones and will resurrect from the dead. Also, the two abodes have been interpreted in association as topological places where souls go after death, to heaven or hell, as the outcome of how we lived, in terms of rewards or punishments in the afterlife.

True, a warning tone sometimes overshadows the *Gathas*. Even a wish for reprisals, more specifically for individuals who adhere to falseness and refuse to open their eyes. Still, it is difficult to tell whether the 'final judgement' is carried out once and for all at the end of our living days or whether wisdom can enter the human heart time and time again, until we breathe our last breath. The generic expression *Memento mori*, remember you must die, does not only reflect the agony of the last moment. It prepares for the moment that lies in wait, to be aware of our finiteness here and now and to grow accustomed to the idea that there are different ways of departing from this early existence.

This is thought-provoking insofar as we are urged to consider the primordial choice described earlier and to arrive at the 'final judgement' in our lives every new day that passes. According to this interpretation which I admit is a personal one, the passage concerning the weigh bridge receives a different orientation. It appears to be more in line with the overall philosophy of the *Gathas*, which is mainly an eye-opener for deceivers, rather than an appeal for reprisals against them. The image of compensation awaiting the good in the afterlife, of being safeguarded from eternal hell, and of terrifying punishments being heaped upon the bad, has caused people to live in function of an imagined instance who hands out the rewards or the punishments. It has been linked to the idea of a sovereign judge, a fearful god, who hopefully does not decide arbitrarily who will be happy and who will be doomed to spend his life or his afterlife in unhappiness.

As stated earlier, Zarathustra inspired his companions to become responsible beings, rather than to rely on the intervention of a divine being to alter their situation. Before it is too late and before falling into apathy, he urged them not to give into old habits and encouraged them to change their behaviour. It is unclear in which later texts the concept of a final account was added, together with that of the 'end of times'. For instance, the idea of the world ultimately being restored to the state it was in at the time of creation was not unfamiliar in later Zoroastrianism. Also, the end of times has been associated with the coming of a Saviour, when all or at least the chosen ones enter the kingdom of heaven and receive eternal life.

The does not alter the fact that the responsibility generated by the prospect of a weigh bridge is connected with doing things on time, before it is too late. For this reason, the 'final judgement' expressed by

Zarathustra depends on us, each single day as it were, on our judgement, preferably in line with cosmic self-regulation. Obviously, we cannot place ourselves in the position of a sovereign power and a sovereign justice, higher than the human concept of justice. But we can try to live in accordance with *asha*, the self-regulating principle to be discovered in nature's ingenuity (see next section).

Hence the importance of good thinking, of good reasoning combined with trust in the events. And of *asha*, considered as an intermediary element, as a link between infinite wisdom and human wisdom[16]. Individuals who, as a result of good thinking, experience the impression of a cosmic regulation, of the existence of a just order, of things being right, this again being linked to a sovereign just power, are not completely separated from this sovereign energy. And this is also the case with the opposite impression of things not being right, of things being out of joint. Zarathustra had the intuition of antithetical principles existing in the human mind and functioning as driving forces and pointed at the possibility of humans to activate the renewable force of becoming more just. This sovereign force was not concentrated in a sovereign figure, but to be found in the regenerative potential of humans who participate in the process.

Finally, the passages on the two abodes include references to the final outcome of one individual in relation to his or her chosen direction. In not associating the two abodes with places we go to after death, they are less

---

16   The idea of an intermediary element is mostly ascribed to Mithra, who is absent in the *Gathas*, but was reintroduced in Mazdeism after Zarathustra. Mithra (with an h) is an Aryan, Indo-Iranian deity who appears in India as Mitra (without h) in an association with Varuna. He reappeared in the post-Gathic Avesta as 'the custodian of the contract. Because of his position as a god of righteousness, he was associated with the sun and it was this image of Mithras (with an s) that was conveyed to Rome. Zarathustra did not resume Mithraic worship probably because he did not recommend animal sacrifice. He may have condemned the practice of spilling blood as a sign of redemption and replaced it by spilling water. The Judeo-Christian baptism can be interpreted in this sense. Water is poured to ensure the purity of the soul, holy water being a form of purification. When the Romans were confronted with Mithraism in the first century BC, Plutarch witnessed strange sacrificial acts. He described Mithra as the mediator between Ormazd and Ahriman. Later, Mithra became *Sol Invictus* for the Romans, at the time when the cult of the sun was gaining the West. In *Mithra et le mithriacisme*, Robert Turcan, observes that in the Roman era, Mithraists claimed that Zarathustra and the Magi were "the holy founders of their mystery liturgy". (Paris, Les Belles Lettres, 1993, pp. 27-28).

representational and can be perceived as alternating periods. In fact, this corresponds better with the time frame of progression and regression. During our lifetime, "we go through weal and woe, which is part of the plan", as is expressed in verse 45,9. In order to progress, humans depend on both misery and joyfulness, progression and regression. And especially, on the capacity to distinguish between the broader picture of progress and personal progression or regression. So, if the wrongdoer, for instance, goes through 'hell' as a metaphor referring to his actual existential state, he is well aware that he is going astray; he knows he is fighting against himself.

These are the two reasons why I choose to postpone the attribution of the final judgement to a God who decides on judgement day. From a monotheistic viewpoint, justice is associated with the existence of an all-knowing intelligence, with the idea of a sovereign judgement by the figure of an impartial judge, with one god being superior to all others gods. Still, a regular confrontation with infinite wisdom is quite different from a one-time judgement by God as a result of the life one has led. What is totally absent in the *Gathas* is the idea of a sovereign judge who punishes or rewards, Zarathustra being the only one who assumes that "frustration shall the false ones find, while the truthful ones shall be blessed" (51,9). Nothing allows us to confidently claim that there is one last judgement, a last stage, nor that there are unlimited chances to take oneself in hand. At this stage, we may conclude that every time the individual tries to live in accordance with *asha* – through verification by the tripartite motto – the 'final' judgement, at least one-sidedly, is being implemented.

Self-regulation

In the *Gathas*, the dynamic principle, the logic or order guiding progression is called *asha*. As a hypostasis of wisdom, some philologists have preferred not to translate the word, or to connect it to the Vedic *rta* (*arta, rita*), a regulator of all movement. By developing their intellect, humans aim to live in correspondence with the ordering principle of the universe, to follow the ingenuity of the universe that regenerates in them. The very fact that they have an intellect could work as a signal, combined with individual explicit confirmations of the existence of a regulating principle. Indeed, *asha*, as an equivalent of *rta*, becomes a regulator as soon as humans recognise it as such. Once it is reflected in the moral conduct of an individual, it may start to function as a recognisable self-regulating principle.

The idea that everything responds to a universal dynamic on which we can rely was truly revolutionary. Just as lying by itself generates more lies if one does not resist to it, so also does the aspiration to more trueness lead to more trueness and indirectly mobilises others to do the same. As previously stated, the self-regulating principle of trueness reaches its more pronounced form when the human being considers his relations as microcosmic replicas of the macrocosmic dynamism. A cosmic harmony is to be attested in the assumption that not chaos reigns, but an ordering principle. Individuals who are conscious of the two opposed tendencies, the *ashavans*, do not perceive *asha* as a law to abide by, but as a motor, a dynamic regulator that gives an orientation to existence; as a principle of life that makes them wish to be personally involved in a progressive course of events that is also beneficial to the community.

For a good understanding of the concept of *asha*, let us consider the various translations that have been proposed. The assimilation of *asha* with 'justice' or 'righteousness' has not been withheld in this book. Some translators have opted for 'truth', and Gherardo Gnoli states that *asha* was already present in the pre-Mazdean religions as a truth acquired by means of initiation. He underlines that the *ashavans*, 'possessors of truth', through rituals entered into a new stage of existence. Gnoli rightly underlines that purification rituals undoubtedly had an important function in the process of becoming a 'possessor of truth'[17]. What is problematic however in the concept of truth is that it evokes the idea of telling the truth. We cannot emphasise enough that the opposition of 'the truth' and 'the lie' (*asha* and *druj*, and respectively the truth-teller and the liar, *ashavan* and *dregvant*) is not just about the fight against the inclination to lie. Zarathustra is not discussing the hesitation between telling the truth and lying; he is choosing truth over the lie, being true over being deceitful. Dealing with the truth is not limited to issuing statements which prove to be accurate or incorrect. If "a lie is a destroyer of life" (53.6), it is because a dishonest life does not make us happy, and not because we have failed to tell the truth.

Next to 'truth', *logos* has been proposed as a good equivalent for *asha*. In the Greek philosophers' tradition, *logos* was linked to a logic that dominates the universe, as in the philosophy of Heraclitus for instance.

---

17   Gherardo Gnoli, 'Le religioni dell'Iran antico e Zoroastro', in *Storia delle religioni*, Giovanni Filorama (ed. Vol I, Rome and Bari, Laterza, 1994, p. 356 and p.469).

Polemos, the struggle of opposite forces, is regulated by an ordering principle[18]. However, this law of nature or cosmic intellect was seen as something inevitable. Most Greek philosophers clung to it as a kind of necessity or fate (*moira, ananké*). Even Pythagorean harmony, as the law of numbers, was conceived as a static, immutable and divine order, one that does not really stimulate the responsibility of men. In fact, the Greek philosophers remained submissive to the Greek deities. Divine reason was attributed to deified men who overpowered and yielded to the arbitrary will of a hierarchical pantheon. Pythagoras believed that man can take part in the reign of the immortal gods and be less submitted to fate, an idea that was taken over by the Pythagoreans in southern Italy.

The latter idea corresponds more with Zarathustra's thoughts on humans who should not seek to master the world by defending the loyal servitude to certain divinities. Still, Zarathustra did not perceive the universe as a static, harmonic cosmos, and used a language expressing the progressive dynamics towards completion. Different from Greek *logos*, a static law of nature[19], *asha* can also be discovered within, in an ongoing process allowing humans to activate their inborn potential in line with cosmic dynamism. So, preference is given to the connotation of *asha* with 'true order' – rather than 'good order', the order of how things should be -, emphasising what really takes place in a given situation. This brings us closer to the idea of 'the self-regulation of trueness'. Seen from this angle, *true* and *real* are more accurate expressions than 'the truth'.

In terms of a reality-check, the use of expressions like 'being true' differ from 'the truth'. The adjectives 'real' and 'true' (similar to *echt* and *wahr* in German) are different from the substantive 'truth' (just like *vrai* differs from *la vérité* in French). Trueness, rather than 'the truth', seems more appropriate, because it is less tied to definitions and explanations, to verbal convictions, given the focus on what actually occurs, the tripartite motto

---

18 Diogenes Laertius mentions that there was a correspondence between Heraclitus and Darius I. Heraclitus, who had a more dynamic view of the cosmic laws than Pythagoras, was the first to use the concept of *logos*. Not only did he underline the struggle between opposite forces and the perpetual becoming of everything (*panta rhei*), he also considered fire to be a primal principle (*Lives of eminent philosophers*, Book IX).

19 The Stoic concept of *logos* comes close to a just law of nature, given that nature is gifted with an inborn intelligence that can be discovered by the human intellect. To hold to the idea that the cosmos is put in perfect order by right reason inspired the Stoics to live in agreement with the cosmos.

helping to determine to what extent we follow the truer or less true path. Of course, perception will always play its role, but each person involved in the constant attempt to try and weigh carefully in how far the tripartite motto can be followed will also depend on his fellow men and on the practice of mutual trust. The motto only makes sense to people who are "led by the tendency towards trueness and by good thinking, led by thought and words and deeds through the self-regulation (47,1). Including those who are "led by the tendency towards trueness to the best (…), having only Mazda as the father of self-regulation" (47,2).

Cosmodicy

Based on the definition of theodicy, the term cosmodicy identifies the fundamental goodness of the universe. Its justification can be found in the idea that the ways of the universe are fundamentally good. Evil and suffering are as such perceived by humans, but they hide another world which is imperceptible. While a theodicy is founded on the idea that God is good and works in mysterious ways, a cosmodicy implies that everything that happens is ultimately for the best. On the basis of two assumptions, we could argue that the Gathic vision contains a first draft of a cosmodicy with a theodicean dimension: the dynamic self-regulation is desired and known by Ahura Mazda, who is both personified and not personified by Zarathustra; and the whole of creation responds to *asha*. The fundamental goodness of the universe is an act of its creator, with this valuable addition that a perfect cosmos depends on humans who accept responsibility for their deeds. Zarathustra's trust in the course of things thus depends on the good understanding of man's place in the world.

Instead of trying to explain how evil and suffering entered the world, Zarathustra makes us understand that the cosmos is perfectly created, but that it is unfinished and that humans are responsible for bad things happening if they don't engage in the divine plan and leave the work unfinished. An important step forward is made by no longer ascribing human suffering to the planets, the stars, or the gods. Instead of instilling guilt or fear in the heart of humans, the cooperation with the ingenious cosmic self-regulating principle is stimulated. So, an appeal is made to humans to assume their responsibility in making wise choices and to perform rituals as an essential part of entering the cosmic play. Rituals indeed constitute supporting and strengthening elements in the contact with life's energy.

Mircea Eliade states that the creation of the world is symbolically imitated through all kinds of rituals such as the recitation of sacred texts and in the celebration of important events for individuals or for the collectivity. He observes that every year, the symbolic destruction of the world is ritually performed and the archetypical gesture of creation is imitated[20]. To be added here is the importance of the act of creation being imbued with a sense of divine friendship, with the love for infinite wisdom, which enhances the human freedom to cooperate in the process that has remained unaccomplished.

Now, human freedom of choice leaves each individual free to cooperate or not. The co-worker of wisdom, as stated before, is based on the underlying idea that everything evolves for the best. In a cosmodicy, individuals become co-workers and co-creators of the masterpiece on the basis of the conception that each individual life is an archetypical model of life itself. Hence the conviction that humans engage individually in their activities in the assumption that they are cooperating to a common project. Most innovating is therefore the vision that everything follows a universal dynamism in which we can all put our trust. How reassuring it must have been to discover the possibility of learning how to cross the different thresholds of anguish, how not to be crushed by arbitrary laws and how to be part of a structured universe in which one develops one's personality and blossoms together with others. We might consider this pre-disciplinary holism as a naive belief, as a 'magical' intuition, invented by thinkers who were very close to the life they lived, but the holistic vision inspired them to constantly refine their intuition.

The reader of the *Gathas* recognises the embryonic elements of what will be elaborated in the cosmologies of later philosophical texts. Of course, proto-philosophical texts have the disadvantage of there not being a critical mind-set. To be a lover of wisdom in those days meant that intellect and experience were very much intertwined, that the critical eye was inherent to practice. No one other than Plato stated that Greek thinking was superior to that of the Barbarians[21]. At the same time, he was aware of the risk implied in wisdom becoming no more than a theory that

---

20   Mircea Eliade, *Mythes, rêves et mystères* (Paris, Gallimard, 1959, pp. 202-203).
21   In the Supplement to the Laws or *Epinomis* (986 e), Plato refers to Zarathustra (although he does not mention his name "because he was a Barbarian"), who was the first man to have observed the celestial bodies.

can be put to practice, thereby provoking a shift in education. During the period of the Sophists in Ancient Greece, cerebral capacity and reasoned calculation led to the triumph of rhetoric. A warning had already been expressed by Zarathustra who was most suspicious of the oratorical success of leaders who abuse the power of words. Plato, who knew and defended the tripartite motto, could himself ascertain how often thinking is separated from the way of life (see part IV).

Progression

The liberating message of Zarathustra is to achieve the purpose of creation, which is why he urged humans to consider the "final account" (31,14). I read this as an instigation to set things right while there is time. Zarathustra emphasised the regret for not having made better choices when it was still possible. His whole philosophy is focused on progression, on finding "the best existence" (30,4) on time. The warnings he expressed are fundamentally different from the warning to refrain from earthly pleasures, the detachment from the body through abstinence, in a strict lifestyle according to the logic of sacrifice and self-sacrifice. Again, there is no mention of freeing the soul from the body. Trying to free the soul so that we have the guarantee it will definitely leave the body in the afterlife is only predominant in religions that essentially promote abstinence from carnal pleasure. Rather than the liberation of the soul from the corporeal in ascetic lifestyles, the two kinds of existence that are evoked have everything to do with the aforementioned life and non-life.

By inventing ascetic rules of life that automatically lead to violations and trespassing because they are by definition impossible to observe, it happens that a sense of guilt is developed, and along with it, the impression that we deserve punishments. Instead of cultivating a sense of guilt, with punishment or mortification as a result, the Zoroastrian way of life is about examining yourself in what causes you sadness. It is not about self-sacrifice. The frustrations caused by the denial of life, when people sacrifice themselves which in no way favours fulfilment, too often result in a destroyed future[22]. One of the best-known pitfalls of thought is indeed

---

22 In Lacanian psychoanalysis, the obscure desire to sacrifice is analysed as "something to which few subjects do not succumb, in a monstrous capture" (*Le Seminaire*, Book XI). It is the dependence on the absolute Other that creates

guilt, especially when self-esteem is crushed and a long exculpation process seems necessary. Sometimes guilt can hardly be eliminated when it has been imparted at a young age. Each time a person desperately tries to oppose it, it resurfaces and exerts its paralyzing power.

Surprisingly, Zoroastrians do not support the idea of guilt[23]. Instead of guilt or innocence being the frame of thought, instead of blaming a person for their mistakes, they suggest an empowerment without guilt. Rather than charging oneself to gain purity and starting with a blank page, we recognise our shortcomings and are prepared to work on them. Unlike trying to achieve an unburdened and clear conscience, we recognise our wrongdoings and are ready to address them. This way, there can be no reason for self-disparagement and humiliation, but strength divine is invoked. Strength, forcefulness come from following the true order of existence and Zarathustra highlighted the regeneration process on the basis of free choice. He did not invoke threats, but warned against the misuse of infinite generosity.

Not guilt was imparted by Zarathustra, but rather the adverse consequences of bad choices, one of which is regret. So, no progression is possible if a majority of fellow-citizens neglect the primal scream. When humans "prevent all growth in life" and are being "dragged away from the true self" (53,6), because they failed to understand "the merits of true life" (53,7) on time, then a final moment will come that erring souls cannot be saved and "in the abode of untruth shall they dwell" (51,14). The 'final judgement' is thus associated with the ultimate moment of regret in the statement that the disciples of trueness will reach the best existence, while a poor existence awaits the followers of deceit (30,4).

---

the willingness to sacrifice. In the attitude of devotion and idolatry resonates the desire to renounce something. The will to sacrifice and asceticism go hand-in-hand with self-abnegation and self-denial. According to Lacan, dependence will never be transformed into independence. Our being subject to the desire of the Other is double.

23 A. Govindacharya Svamin observes (although there is no evidence for these assertions) that Mazdeans were already present in India before their migration to Iran and that the Zoroastrians returned to India in 732 BC. He considers the fire ceremony as a common heritage of the Brahmanas and states that Vishnuism is the fulfilment of Mazdeism (p. 63). Note this remark on the absence of punishments and on the alternative to 'rearrange' or 'readjust' when something is out of order. *Mazdaism in the light of Vishnuism* (Mysore, GTA, 1913, pp. 2-12).

From the beginning, Zarathustra's warning was directed against those who ignore the divine plan and are "voluntarily deaf" (32,12); they think of themselves as victorious, when in fact, they are "victims, damned to slavery" (32,15). To prevent them from living their last days in regret, and before it became too late for them to be saved, he pointed to the miserable end they were heading for.

No one can expect that endless possibilities are offered to adjust one's way of life. Those who "have been all the time in the abode of deceit" (46,11) will not suddenly be exempt by an act of grace. "Wherever the spirit of the followers of untruth prevails (...) grief and regret shall be your end" (53,7), observed Zarathustra. So, he declared to his companions: "I will give my friendship and warmth to he who joins me" (46,13). He was urging men and women, with determination, to guide themselves towards a truer self, to a point where they no longer allow themselves to act in a thoughtless manner and do harm to creation. Again, he was seeking to awaken their thoughts, to prevent individuals from becoming aware of their errors too late, when at the end nothing is left but regret.

New times

Implicit in the *Gathas* is the idea that better times lie ahead, which makes people not give up and persevere. Actually, to become aware of a creative inner energy is likely to create a good mind. As discussed in previous chapters, the announcement of glad tidings engendered a new concept of existence. And this again was linked to a new concept of time. What needs to be specified is that the glad tidings are not to be seen as a guarantee. The good news Zarathustra brings is not about a magical, ever succeeding happiness being just around the corner, as is clear in: "Only hard and relentless work can lead to the understanding of one's inner strength in order to use it for a better life" (51,19).

If no 'end of times' can be found in the *Gathas*, the underlying concept is rather that of 'new times', of renovated attempts to stop inflicted injustices, to come clear with oneself. In mobilising his companions, paralysed by fatalism, Zarathustra tried to convince them of their potential to put an end to their non-life, a capacity present in each individual. But since progression in life does not necessarily correspond to the human logic of a beginning and an end, and because striving to achieve one's goal is often much more difficult than anticipated, he must have made them reconsider and open up to a more discontinuous approach. One cannot help wondering to what degree the utopia of prosperous times ahead actually instigated the companions to evaluate their actions over and over again. Otherwise stated, in making abstraction of a continuous process, could his companions come to the understanding that life is not linear, but consists of progression and regression; that it is made of periods and episodes?

New in the *Gathas* is indeed the concept of time, implying a progression towards completion, be it in a discontinuous way. By the grace of time so to speak, we can become acquainted with the dynamic vision of progression and regression, and not less with the unfinished work and its possible realisation in time. No responsibility can be induced if time is endless, if we are not in a position to look ahead from a given perspective, namely that of our changing relation to the two tendencies. By urging his listeners to think for themselves, Zarathustra may possibly have observed that they became familiar with the concept of new times and discovered the growing awareness of mutual cooperation. The introduction of 'new times', of a 'new day' may have enhanced the personal implication in a given course of events. Maybe in being their own supreme judge of persisting on the path of trueness, they found friends on the way who also resisted false pretenses; friends who no longer listened to those who "turn aside the minds of righteous men", who "through their teaching try their very best that men may leave the honest path of work" (32,11-12).

Increasingly predominant must have been the new concept of time that made people aware of their possible involvement in the evolutionary process and of the generosity of infinite wisdom that can generate gratitude. At least, this is how I analyse the concept of time, and more importantly, the evolution of how the idea of a new beginning could emerge. There is indeed this one new element we cannot overlook, namely the possibility of prospection, of looking ahead, of time coming. Zarathustra seems to have invented hope in his chants, leaving the impression that there is time, till the final breath, to set things right. Paradoxically, in order to present the idea of a future, he appears to have clung to the idea that there is necessarily a limit imposed to human action. Indeed, to imagine being dead tomorrow makes us realise what is most necessary today. Do not put off until tomorrow to become the person you can be today is what our finiteness tells us. To be mortal is not necessarily threatening, but something life needs, conveying a capacity to live, meaning that if life is finite, we can consider it as conferring a life force, much greater than the fear of death. A fading fear of death can be ascribed to the self-regulating process that installs a serenity in man[24].

In sum, there is no frightening end of times, no mention in the *Gathas* of an apocalyptic or eschatological event, no promise of a Saviour coming to deliver the righteous and to send the sinners to hell, but a prudent prognostic of new times, of a new perspective on existence. Yet, some scholars have characterised Zoroastrianism as an eschatology, a theory on the last things[25]. They advance the idea that the 'end of times' implies that good will conquer evil. This may imply there is an end to earthly suffering, that each existence can come to completion, or that perfection awaits humanity. As others have pointed out before me, the Gathic expression of *saoshyant* or liberator has been interpreted in a messianic way[26]. Still, if I am not mistaken, the implied progression toward completion is not to be assimilated with one *Saoshyant*, with a capital S, especially if this induces the impression that we patiently await a divine intervention. "The wisdom of *saoshyants* shining forth shall teach mankind effectively to speed", declares Zarathustra (46,3). *Saoshyants* or liberators are the adversaries of untrueness; those who can liberate the creative force inside. They are blessed with the gift of being able to liberate the light that shines in darkness and guide others in their progression to a fulfilling community life.

---

24 It reminds us of the German philosopher Rainer Marten who argues that, instead of being repudiated by death, we can "love our own death" (*Der menschliche* Tod, Freiburg/München, Karl Alber, 2016, 15). By entering into a relation with it as "something not completely foreign, aggressive and destructive", to die and to let death come implies a kind of self-respect. The capacity to die, according to Marten, is inseparable from the finding that we did not yet completely do the most necessary in life.
25 Especially in Bundahisn (6th to 11th centuries, based on knowledge derived from the Zend), there is the idea of an eschatological transfiguration of the world. Eventually, everybody will go to paradise but first, sinners must be purified and released, and hell itself must be purified and burned. When the time is right for the cosmic conflict, even hell will be encapsulated within the cosmic order.
26 The Messianic overtone of a single saviour is not discordant with the way in which the term develops in later Avestan texts. Jenny Rose notes that the term appears six times in the Gathas, referring to 'one who will be strong' or 'one who will revitalize'. It occurs three times in the plural, indicating that "the future of this figure may be construed in broad general termes" (*Zoroastrianism: An Introduction*, London/New York, Tauris, 2011, p. 23).

Regeneration

Zarathustra's name stands for the constant regeneration of what is life-giving[27]. Regeneration, as I understand from the *Gathas,* is the key motive in Zarathustra's existential philosophy. Firstly, he wishes to awaken humanity, a topic of all times, and to revive the initial potential of every human being. Secondly, what has been generated before us – and also for us – can by regenerated by us. That is, by individuals who recognise the regenerative power in which they participate. Thirdly, regeneration only makes sense to the human mind when life is not pointless, when it is not perceived as a cynical waste of efforts, as a fatalistic reaction to a chain of events that humans cannot understand or by which they are totally subjugated.

Now, we are told that intuitive strengthening is implied in the regenerative process and that it is based on the idea that human nature participates in a vital motion. The evolution of mankind consists of contributing to the dynamism of life and to making all things evolve through a regenerative power. Pointing to this vitalizing potential, Zarathustra exclaimed: "Teach me, O Mazda [...] how I can regenerate my life and make it true" (34,15). The main condition to find a connection with wisdom within apparently lies in the capacity to nourish the natural potential that makes all creatures grow. This is not a one-time operation, implying a spiritual opening to a divinity and making it last for an entire lifetime, which is why two considerations are in order.

The inner universe, similar to outer space, is ever evolving and depends on humans who follow the luminous path to the truest in order to reach the supreme good (43,3). The orientation that Zarathustra invites us to adopt is to regenerate the social dimension in the mutual endeavour to achieve sound relationships. As stated before, the friend and the foe in our inner selves who seem to lead a secret life, come to the surface and have an indirect impact on our relations with others in the process of opening up to more consistency. The confrontation of the inner friend and enemy – sometimes by admitting we are at war with ourselves – is obviously not intended to

---

[27] Prods Oktor Skjaervo states that the underlying theme of the Old Avestan text is revitalising strength and that it refers to Ahura Mazda as the healer of existence. https://sites.fas.harvard.edu/~iranian/Zoroastrianism/Zoroastrianism1_Intro.pdf

create categories of friends and enemies in our relationships. The ability to recognise the two opposite tendencies and to support the friend against the enemy has the function to activate the faculty of responsibility. Its implicit social dimension is intended to make us re-evaluate our social life and to open up to otherness.

Moreover, it sometimes happens that we simply do not have the strength to face the paralyzing effect of the inner contradictions in the depths of our human hearts. However much we see ourselves as being the living scene of internal quarrels, the mere will to put an end to the internal strife has no decisive power. The strength to have an open mind, the confidence comes from elsewhere, especially when the primordial choice unleashes the power to prioritise the friend. "With the assistance of good thinking, let strength (*khshathra*) come to us for the advancement of humanity" (45,9), says Zarathustra. This line is on the readiness to open up to the internal conflict and to the driving life force stimulating even more openness. Highlighted is the faculty of opening up to the friend which can release an unexpected energy. Otherwise stated, the opening up to the confidant releases an unexpected energy coming from the confidant. The liberating effect seems to manifest itself autonomously, almost without any effort on our part: "Wisdom and good thinking bring strength to serve (...) our souls grow strong, our lives renewed" (45,10). This is how a regenerative potential can make its appearance from the inner conflict. The wish to promote trueness makes us discover an interactive mechanism between our openness and that of others.

It is generally agreed that we cannot eliminate wrong deeds by doing wrong, and neither should we do wrong towards wrongdoers. The only way to ensure that we do not generate more wrong is to depend on the regeneration of the tendency to trueness to be activated. And also in each other, in individuals who understand that conflicts are not necessarily destructive and can generate new perspectives. I refer here to the Chinese word 'crisis' composed of the two elements of danger and opportunity. Obviously, no permanent condition of being in contact with the sovereign rhythms of alive interactions can be acquired; we can only witness the rather rare magical correspondence with the ingenuity of nature. Regenerating forces are highly sophisticated, discontinuous, secret. This is a structural finding that Zarathustra has placed at the centre of our attention, without infringement upon our responsibility.

Completeness

To all those who are in doubt, Zarathustra expressed this encouragement: "Within the space of this one life on earth, completeness can be reached by fervent souls" (51,12). This notion of completeness *(haurvatat)* – also translated as wholeness or perfection, and linked to that of non-deathness *(ameretat)*, also translated as immortality – is about being involved in and committed to the continuous regeneration of an initiated movement. The regeneration process is linked to the idea of eternal life, or better, 'endless light', which does not so much imply the liberation of the soul of the corporeal, but the progression towards accomplishment of what never completely vanishes. As Aristotle pointed out "nature does nothing in vain", everything that comes to exist will develop itself in conformity to its nature.

Let us be clear, when a living being has come to completion, it has reached a state of 'freedom', of no longer being bound to the conditions of life. This is where the *Gathas* deliver interesting insights into the period before death, into how we lived, which will impinge on how we die. The state of being we can find ourselves in at the time of our death, invites us to reflect on the different paths we can follow during our life. This is the reflection I wish to emphasise, without however adding further speculations. What was later referred to as the 'art of dying', *ars moriendi*, is present in the *Gathas*, under the form of a lifelong learning process. Zarathustra engages in the divine project of accelerating wisdom and links the two states of living and dying in order to stimulate us to achieve insight, preferably before it is too late.

The progression towards accomplishment corresponds to the universal principle of regeneration. As discussed in previous chapters, it is the evolving and dynamic aspect of progression that we need to underline. This is somewhat different from a generalised final point, similar to what can be found in the mindset of the three Abrahamic religions. Only when humans feel their actions are leading somewhere, possibly to something greater than themselves, be it the making of an object or the progression towards a goal, will they feel ready to engage in the process – especially when they come to realise that their personal involvement may end sooner than they expect. No one will start something today knowing there is no tomorrow. And even if a plan fails or falls short of expectations, the idea of its possible accomplishment will have been the inspiring element. This anticipated future tense expresses the passion of bringing something to fulfilment that was the initial motivation.

The evolving aspect of the regenerative process in the *Gathas* was translated by Dina McIntyre as the condition of being 'whole, complete' (*haurvatat*)[28]. With regard to existence, completeness is a state humans are capable of achieving as the consequence of a maintained and ordered life, following infinite wisdom. McIntyre did not opt for 'wholeness', the usual translation of *haurvatat*, which is a welcome suggestion, because there is no reason to import the connotation of healing or making healthy. Not so much an unhealthy lifestyle is to be dealt with, but the state of what has not yet reached completion, pointing to a future that makes sense. When for instance a work of art is completed and has reached perfection, the artist puts the final touch, meaning he can leave it alone and let it be.

McIntyre's proposition to connect completeness (*haurvatat*) and non-deathness (*ameretat*) is interesting from the point of view that the daily effort to awaken good thinking, to follow the true order of existence, leads to "a state of being that is not bound to mortality". Although scholars have translated *ameretat* as 'immortality' or 'continuing life', McIntyre wishes to stress "a state of being that is not bound to the conditions of life on earth", that is "unbound from mortality". She seems to underline the state of non-deathness as being exempt from the cyclic play of degeneration and regeneration, necessary to reach a state of completeness or perfection. The mentioned 'state of being' suggests a speculation on death as the relocation of the soul, not necessarily similar to Plato's liberation from the body, from the tomb and prison for the soul, but as a reaching of the light. The state of completeness a human being can find is probably based on verses like these: "To reach where Mazda Ahura reigns" (33,5) or "The goal of life: entrance in your abode" (50,7).

If we agree that contemplation of the divine, according to Zarathustra, does not urge detachment from the material world, but on the contrary, requires knowledge of and desire for wisdom, then the accomplishment of the divine workings cannot be attained without the human contribution. What counts is not so much where we go after death, an expression implying an ongoing progress, but the passion to go through the process with as little regret as possible, by "seeking all ways to foster life" (51,5). Death does not imply a salvation from the world, rather a salvation for the world, meaning that the lifelong

---

28 Earlier mentioned website of Dina McIntyre.

learning process bears fruit also for the other living beings and is of benefit of the future regenerative process. The degree of perfection we reach when our life ends – *perficere*, to complete or finish through doing, *per* (through) *facere* (make, do) – does not refer to excellence, but to the quality of fulfilment. Exactly because of this reason do I wish to stress the notion perfectibility, the evolution towards completion in the progression towards accomplishment.

From East to West?

The global evolutionary theory implied in Zoroastrian thinking, leading to the fulfilment of all creation, is surely impressive. It is difficult to tell when and where it first appeared, since the Indo-European prospect of reaching one's full potential arose in other cultures as well. On numerous occasions in the history of humanity, the name of Zarathustra functioned as a tool, as an inspiring and stimulating idea to achieve what was convenient in different ages. The next chapters focus on the expressed wish to lead humans to happiness, which has been inspirational to the three monotheistic religions and to philosophers in the East and the West. More recent examples of an explicit progression of humanity can be found in the presentations of a divine plan (Teilhard de Chardin), of nature's plan (Darwin), of an anti-Darwinist plan (Nietzsche).

As it happens, the prospect of humanity coming to completion reappeared in the rebirth, literally 'renaissance' of Zoroastrian thinking in Italy. The rebirth of oriental light guaranteed the right orientation. To the Florentine scholars, the image of man presented by Zarathustra favoured the evolution towards the blooming of humanity. This was, for instance, reflected in the expression by Marcilio Ficino of the "flower of intelligence". Influenced by the references of Greek philosophers to the magic of Zarathustra, Ficino states: "Zoroaster names flower of intelligence the very centre of the soul". He recommended listening to the great Persian: "There is something intelligible that you have to understand by the flower of intelligence[29].

---

29 The idea of an intellectual continuum between the East and the West is developed by Cynthia Fleury on whose study I base my own work. As if Ficino had been able to consult the *Gathas*, he evokes divine furore and the function of light as an emancipatory element. He refers to Zarathustra as the 'father of lights', with a Neoplatonist touch, to the light of lights. See *Dialoguer avec l'Orient* (Paris, PUF, 2003, p. 108).

This way, an intellectual continuum was ensured by the transmission of universalist ideas (see part IV).

An admirable overview of the transfer of ideas between Eastern and Western thinking during the Renaissance period can be found in *Dialogue with the Orient* by Cynthia Fleury[30]. This French philosopher proves that during the Italian Renaissance, the East and the West were not as isolated as it is assumed today. Fleury goes back to the period of Persian Renaissance during which the Greek heritage was fortunately apprehended. As a matter of fact, Persian Renaissance took place three centuries before Italian Renaissance. Although she does not include Zoroastrianism in her study, she states that "the intellectual humus is that of a continuum" and proposes the use of the term 'meta-history' to refer to the revival and reactivation of past philosophies in a dialogue with the present.

To summarize, Zarathustra was propelled onto the battlefield between the Persian Neoplatonists and the European Aristotelians. He offered a good alternative to the Byzantine thinkers, who preferred Greek philosophy to the Christian doctrine. The idea of a direct filiation between the East and the West was attested by Byzantine thinker Georges Gemistus Pletho, who put forward the golden link between Zarathustra and Plato. Of course, in those days, nobody had access to the Gathic texts, but thanks to a figure like Pletho, a linear evolution was traced under the form of an underground vein linking the East and the West, even under the form of a golden chain through the ages. Let us add that the proto-philosophy of Zarathustra was also explicitly picked up by the Muslims, especially under the Abbasside rule in Iran (from the 8th to the 13th century). Nor should we forget that the Muslims had access to Greek thought, translated it, commented it, and reactivated it. They were at the origin of the transmission towards medieval European universities. They developed their own theology (in the confrontation with Judaism and Christianity), together with philosophy (*falsafa*). Without ever admitting it, the Muslims are indebted to Persian knowledge[31].

---

30 Fleury makes the point that "the Persian and Florentine Renaissance", each one in their own way, assigned an important role to the philosopher who takes on the responsibility of the 'act of being reborn which is inseparable from the act of praising: "To praise is to live, and to live is to praise" affirms Fleury (2003, 194). The following quotation is on p. 39.

31 See further Part IV. Indeed, many Muslims were Persian. For instance, Al-Ma'mun, the Abbasid who founded the 'House of Wisdom' in Baghdad had a

The following historical overview gives evidence that Zarathustra's name functioned as an axis round which Italian Renaissance came to flourish, and that from the eighteenth century onwards he became an important anticlerical instrument in the virulent attack against the power of the Church of Rome. Later on, he was the 'magical' inspirer of German romanticism in its opposition against rational Cartesianism that left the world disenchanted and without a soul. All of this before Nietzsche created his mythical, heroic figure seeking to find an answer to Western decadence. Surely, very little of the Gathic principles can textually be found in Nietzschean philosophy. Yet, a specific existential line of thinking links the two Zarathustras.

Persian mother. He staffed the academy with graduates from the great Sasanian 'university' of Gundeshapur.

PART FOUR
WHERE?

Zoroastrian heritage?

It is certainly not the purpose of this study to claim the paternity for Greek philosophy. We can however read the texts of Greek philosophers and identify some of the elements that were already dear to Zarathustra. The idea is not new, but what is less talked about is that the roots of Western civilization, which are usually situated in Greece, can be found in the East. If the Zoroastrian heritage is sometimes presented in terms of a direct transition from one continent to the other, this was most obviously the case during the period of the Babylonian exile, when the Jews of Jerusalem were deported by the Assyrians, and liberated by the Persian king Cyrus II (in 538 BC) with the mission to reconstruct in their country of origin the temple of Jerusalem[1].

This was also the case from the 4th century BC onwards when the Persian Empire was conquered by the Macedonian Greeks. The Achaemenid Empire stretched from India to Egypt/Libya and present-day Turkey, and lasted from the sixth century BC till the victory of Alexander the Great in 330 (death of Darius III, destruction of Persepolis). Some of the Greek philosophers believed Zoroaster lived at the pivotal era of Confucius and Buddha and concluded that he was a contemporary thinker, living in the Western part of Persia. Indeed, the first Greek 'philosophers of nature', Thales, Anaximander, Heraclitus, Democritus, took the Magi in Asia Minor as emigrated disciples of Zoroaster, who was presented as the master of Pythagoras. It was understood that he lived in that time, no earlier than the seventh-sixth century BC.

---

1   Jan Assman refers to the solidarity between Achaemenid Zoroastrianism of the 6th century BC and Judaism. Not only did Cyrus reconstruct the temple of Jerusalem, Assman also mentions the construction by Darius I of an Amon temple in the oasis of El Charga. *Moses the Egyptian. The Memory of Egypt in Western Monotheism* (Cambridge, Harvard University Press, 1997).

In fact, Pythagoras remained in Babylon for twelve years and knew of the wisdom of the Magi. He is said to have travelled all the way through Persia and reached India, where he learned about the theory of reincarnation. His ideas influenced well-known philosophers such as Plato and Aristotle in the fourth century BC, who at that time were interested in Persian virtues like freedom, equality, friendship. In fact, Greek philosophy was not created out of nothing and it did not develop in a vacuum. Ancient Greece owed a lot to Persian antiquity and to oriental wisdom that had emerged centuries earlier[2].

The idea of a *logos*, a law of nature, a divine order, penetrated in Greek philosophy in its emancipation from mythology. The Greek pantheon consisted of gods and goddesses who were idealized men and women, with superhuman powers who presided over human fate. The predominant fatalism in mythology left its mark on Greek philosophy, especially on the first school of the 'philosophers of nature' in Asia Minor. The word *logos*, used in different ways, was considered in Greek cosmology as an ordering principle implicit in the cosmos. It was conceived as a perfect order that gave form to nature, impregnated of beauty and harmony. When contemplating the earth and sky, one can easily see the divine touch in the primal disorder or chaos. Only the Greek Stoics assimilated *logos* with a generative principle of the universe. This comes close to Zoroastrian cosmology, with its equivalent *asha*. The great discovery in Zoroastrian cosmology was however the conception of the universe, perfectly designed by a creator, architect or organiser, and depending on humans acting as co-creators to reach perfection.

One should of course not lose sight of the fact that the different visions on the 'origin of thought' are very much intertwined. In short, at the apogee of Greek philosophy, Zarathustra was known both as a reformer and the founder of the religion of the Magi and as an expert in astronomy who had taught the Babylonians. He was even recognised as the founder of sidereal mathematics, long before Pythagoras. Most studies of the Greek historians (see further) were based on the transmission of ideas that took place between 600 and 300 BC. The sages of the Hellenistic period valued the wisdom of Zarathustra. They argued all sciences stemmed from him.

---

2   For further reading see J. Bidez et F. Cumont, *Les Mages hellénisés, Zoroastre, Ostanès et Hystaspe d'après la tradition grecque* (Paris, Les Belles Lettres, 1973); M.I. West, *Early Greek Philosophy and the Orient* (Oxford, Clarendon Press (2002); A.F. de Jong, *Traditions of the Magi: Zoroastrianism in Greek and Latin Literature* (Leiden, Brill, 1997).

While some of them wanted to pay tribute to the grand sage, others tried to appropriate his thinking and achieve individual gain. The more his name gained in reputation, the more often the conceptions stemming from the East were distorted.

Middle East and Egypt

Since the 4th century BC, Syria was the land of many Hellenized Magi. Paul Du Breuil maintains that there was a rich literature on Zarathustra of a Chaldean nature[3]. Many Magi had travelled towards the West in the wake of the Persian army and their continual mobility made true nomads of them. A sect of Western Magi known as Maguseans, emigrated Iranians affiliated to the *magus*, settled on the western side of the Euphrates river. After the victory of the Greeks over the Persians, a large number of wise men reached Syria, which explains the presence of a Chaldean Zarathustra in the Syrian tradition.

Later, after the wars against the Romans, the Iranian wise men travelled to Asia Minor. Since Parthian Iran was an ally of Judah in the war against the Romans, the earlier established ties were thus reinforced. According to Du Breuil, the Essenes – one of the three most important 'sects', next to the Pharisees and the Sadducees who lived in Palestine and in the Roman province of Syria – hoped for the return of the Persians. They hoped the latter would chase the Romans and re-establish a new Israel. A shared spirituality contributed to this evolution. The Partho-Roman war did not harm the esoteric contacts between the Essenes and the Magi, who conveyed so many Mago-Zoroastrian concepts.

On the contrary, in the second century BC, apocalyptic scriptures of a Mazdeo-Zoroastrian nature circulated in the Middle East. A well-known example is that of the Magi heading towards Bethlehem, a most important episode inspired by the relations with Magi in the first century BC. An apocryphal form of literature in Greek known as the Oracles of Hystapes – the king Vishtaspa mentioned in the *Gathas* – had resonated among the Essenes who adopted a solar culture and practised a ritual at sunrise, a gesture of veneration to the divine light. Du Breuil's conclusion was that the Gathic thought survived until the Essenes[4].

---

3   See Du Breuil (1978, 292 ff).
4   Du Breuil (1978, 296).

Second order texts bearing witness to the work of Zarathustra and to the Magi started to circulate freely in the first centuries AD. Though impossible to substantiate, the belief was that a substantial part of Persian wisdom was conserved in the library of Alexandria in Egypt. The library was famous for the conservation of thousands of scrolls containing ancient knowledge. About 800 of these scrolls were attributed to Zarathustra whose ideas had been written down by the Magi. Hermippus of Smyrna, who worked in Alexandria, is known to have produced a book on "The writings of Zoroaster" around the year 200 BC in which he explained that Greek philosophy had an oriental, magical origin[5]. In those days, the name of Zoroaster was indeed related to a secret doctrine.

A few centuries later, at the beginning of the Christian era, Philo of Alexandria was teaching a kind of universalism that resembled the Zoroastrian doctrine. Philo, a Jewish and Hellenized philosopher, was interested in the pagan cults preceding the tradition of Abraham. He was convinced that the monotheism of Moses was universal and that Christianity was derived from Judaism and Hellenism. According to him, one can perfectly reconcile Jewish faith and Greek philosophy, which by the way was an idea that inspired the Fathers of the Church. Philo translated Judaism in terms of stoic, platonic and neo-Pythagorean elements and he supported the doctrine of the *logos*, with clear parallels to be drawn with Gathic *asha*.

Philo stated that Plato had borrowed his ideas from Moses, whom he considered as the greatest philosopher. According to Philo, Moses was the ideal king-philosopher. He led his people, an enslaving minority, out of Egypt, and became a lawgiver in Israel. Given the fact that Philo represented the Greek-Egyptian tradition of the first century BC, we cannot ignore the important role Egypt played in the filiation of ideas[6]. Though it is not possible to reconstruct the facts, we can however highlight the fact

---

5   I refer to the earlier references in note 8 of my introduction.
6   During the Achaemenid Empire, Cambyses and Darius I were respected and venerated in Egypt. Possibly, an Egyptian influence on Persian culture explains the resemblance of the symbol of Zoroastrianism – the winged disk now referred to as the *faravahar* – and the Egyptian goddess Isis. But also in Mesopotamia the winged disk was associated with deities connected with the sun. The iconography of the Achaemenid period is indeed Assyrian, just like Achaemenid architecture is (e.g. the human-headed winged bull and the column capitals). See Jean Perrot (ed.), *The Palace of Darius at Susa* (London-New York, Tauris, 2013).

that Moses is supposed to have been raised by an Egyptian royal family[7]. Egypt was first a Persian, then a Greek colony. As to the question whether Moses was a legendary figure or a historical person, the fact remains that prophets embody the idealised individuals that appeal to the people. This is also true for Zarathustra.

Zoroastrianism and Judaism

In the 16th century, French and Portuguese travelers (for instance Garcia de Orta) thought that Zoroastrians are Jewish; that they are non-orthodox Jews who preferred not to distinguish themselves through exterior signs. Nothing can be further from the truth. Even though the two people are historically related, the fact remains that they are fundamentally different, by their religion, their historical background, their culture, which is why the historical influence of Judaism on Zoroastrianism, and vice versa, is limited to no more than a number of speculations. Recent studies confirm the influence of Zoroastrianism at a given moment of time when the two religions were in close contact, chiefly during and after the period of the Babylonian exile. Although the Hebrews were liberated by the Persians and were allowed to return to Jerusalem, many stayed in Babylon, where they could freely confess their faith under Persian domination[8].

Even after the conquest by Alexander the Great, they remained faithful to king Darius III. Monique Zetlaouï declares that "the Jewish monotheism becomes Iranian in the contact with the Persians" and that Zoroastrianism corresponded with Hebrew thought[9]. She remarks that in the text preceding the exile, the Jewish God is tribal "attached to his people and to their land". In the later texts "after the encounter with the Persian Empire, Yahweh acquires a more universal dimension". According to Zetlaouï, "the exile

---

7   Jan Assman (1997, 184). The information in this paragraph is based on Assman's study (from p. 88 onwards) that contains an interesting thesis on Moses who divulgated to the Hebrews the elements of Egyptian mystery cults. This means that Hebrew monotheism has its origins in an earlier polytheism, on its way to henotheism and first monotheism in the worship of the sun-god Aton by the pharaoh Akhenaton. Assman suggests Moses was killed by the Hebrews when they discovered this heresy.
8   Lucien Poznanski, *La Chute du temple de Jérusalem* (Bruxelles, Complexe, 1991, p. 21 ff).
9   Monique Zetlaouïe, *Ainsi vont les enfants de Zarathoustra. Parsis de l'Inde et Zartushtis d'Iran* (Paris, Imago, 2003, pp. 30-31).

had engendered new spiritual needs" and the Zoroastrian responses were "bringing hope". The "role of liberator" by the Persians was fundamental and she insists on the generosity implied by the reconstruction – at their expense – of the temple of a foreign religion. This gesture was more in line with the Persian godhead, than with that of the idolatrous peoples who held them in captivity, and this godhead was more in accordance with the Hebrew perception of a non-representational god.

Late 19th century Iranologists like Jackson and Mills confirmed the parallelism between Zoroastrianism and Judaism[10]. Besides the eschatology, these researchers were particularly interested in the theory of angels, paradise and hell, and the final judgement. The Judeo-Christian approach indeed attests of these elements, also of a subtle shift towards a messianic interpretation. The word 'messiah' by the way stems from *mashia'h*, meaning 'one anointed', which refers to the habit of pouring perfumed olive oil on the head of a person who is consecrated to Yahweh. And the Greek word that corresponds to 'messiah' is *khristos*, the name attributed to Jesus (*khrisma* or the act of anointing). As a reminder, the Hebrew messiah has been awaited in Jewish history (in pre-exilic prophetic books, not the Torah, and it is more fully developed during Persian rule and the Hellenistic period) until an undetermined time, while the Christian messiah has already descended on earth as the son of God and he will return at the 'end of time'.

Now, the idea of salvation is not absent from the *Gathas*, but it is not understood as the coming of a Saviour who will redeem God's people and free them from evil. The implicit idea of liberation close to salvation is one of progression towards the perfection of wisdom. The glad tidings implied in these hymns have everything to do with cooperating with the divine plan, with the progression towards "the final goal of life" and "to serve for long years" (33,5). "Ye liberators, help me in my task" (50,7), Zarathustra thus addressed the guardians of freedom; "O Mazda, *asha* and *vohu manah*, liberators", asking them to bring strength. He also invoked *armaiti* to "grant the salvation good thinking brings" (51,2).

---

10   See A.V. Williams Jackson, *Zoroaster: The Prophet of Ancient* Iran (1898). Lawrence H. Mills who studied the influence of the Zoroastrian religion on Jewish thought in the second tome of *Zarathustra and the Greeks* (Leipzig, Brockhaus, 1903) is also the author of a comparative study between the two concepts of *logos* and *asha*: https://opensiuc.lib.siu.edu/cgi/viewcontent.cgi?referer=https://www.google.be/&httpsredir=1&article=1902&context=ocj

One more particular issue concerns the designation of 'first monotheism'. That Zoroastrians could well be considered the first monotheists did not go down well with the Jews. Because the latter also lay claim to the title, there have been unpredictable reactions on their part, including the claim that Zarathustra was a prophet of Israel or the spreading of the assumption that the Avestan documents were forged under the influence of Hellenized Jews[11]. Paul Du Breuil also declares that – especially in the period of the Hellenisation of Judea, Syria and Mesopotamia by the Seleucids – "the Jews saw Abraham as the initiator of Zoroaster". He adds that the influence of religious Iran on Judaism has remained unrecognised for too long, as well as that of the Zoroastrian gnosis on crypto-Judaism and on the post-exile prophets.

Greece

The Greek historian Herodotus (5th century BC) was the first to report on the life of the Persians. He noted that they did not have temples, altars or statues, and that they climbed to the top of the highest mountains to worship their supreme God. Also, that the Magi chanted their theogony while orienting themselves during prayer towards the sun[12]. Before Herodotus, the historian Xanthos of Lydia claimed that the wisdom of the great Iranian preceded that of the Egyptians. Later, Plutarch (1st century AD) stated that the wisest of men distinguished between the better principle of a god as opposed to a demon. Plutarch was fascinated by Iranian cosmogony, specifically the division between the god Oromazes, born from purest light, and the demon Areimanios, comparable to darkness and ignorance. It was Diogenes Laertius (3rd century AD) who declared that Aristotle was aware of the two principles Oromasdes and Areimanios[13].

---

11 For instance, the prophet Ezekiel, who preached at the end of the 6th century BC in Babylonia, was identified as Zarathustra, or Baruch, the secretary of Jeremiah. These were all attempts to include Zarathustra in the Hebrew tradition. See Du Breuil (1978, 236).
12 Herodotus' *Histories* (in nine books), reports in the first volume the victory of Cyrus II and includes some remarks on the Magi.
13 In his Prologue, Laertius mentions a Treatise on the Magi attributed to Aristotle who "tells us that the name Zoroaster, interpreted literally, means 'star-worshipper". He declares that according to Aristotle "the Magi were more ancient than the Egyptians". Aristotle associated the two principles of a 'good demon', called Oromasdes, to Zeus, and of a 'bad demon', called Areimanios, to the Hades. "This is confirmed by Hermippus in his first book on the Magi by Eudoxus

Pliny the elder confirmed in the first century AD that Zarathustra lived in the sixth millennium BC[14]. He relied on the authority of Aristotle, who declared that his master had learned everything from Zarathustra, that according to Aristotle, the philosophy of Plato was a renaissance of the Persian sage's thinking. Pliny sustained that Zarathustra lived in the sixth millennium BC, based on the idea that the world returns to its starting point every 6000 years. Irrespective of this improbable date, there is no doubt that Zoroastrian ideas penetrated the Academy of Plato. Plato himself admired Persian wisdom and declared that the Greeks owe much to that culture and that "they elevated it to a higher perfection"[15].

Already in the third century BC, Colotes, a disciple of Epicurus, declared that he detected plagiarism in the famous "myth of Er" and that Er was none other than Zoroaster. Plato was discredited and accused of having cheated with regard to Persian wisdom. As Saouâd Ayada maintains, it is not far-fetched to detect manifest signs of iranophilia in Plato. According to her, scholars in antiquity had already noticed the absence of the theme of the king-philosopher in Greek conceptions[16]. But what is more, Plato probably acquired knowledge of the Zoroastrian ideas through Pythagorism in Italy and brought the harmonic composition of the soul to the fore, as well as the perfectibility of the soul through the ternary law.

Plato was impressed by this cosmological view and by the Pythagorean science of numbers, especially the concept of tripartition. He considered that for society to be well structured everyone must occupy his natural place and that not power but intelligence must rule. The tripartition in his political theory implied that each citizen occupies the position he is assigned by nature, which is the best possible guarantee for a long-lasting and harmonious republic[17]. The model of this organic and anthropomorphic tripartition was

---

in his *Voyage round the World*, and by Theopompus in the eighth book of his *Philippica*" (*Lives of eminent philosophers*, I, 8).

14 *Natural History,* 30,3. Pliny the elder was one of the thinkers who stated there was more than one Zoroaster and who questioned whether a distinction should be made between them.

15 Plato speaks of what they may have borrowed from the Barbarians (Supplement to the Laws or *Epinomis*, 987 e).

16 Saouâd Ayada, *L'Islam des théophanies. Une religion à l'épreuve de l'art* (Paris, CNRS, 2010, pp. 210-212).

17 According to Plato, the soul is constituted of three parts that correspond to the three parts of the body; the head, heart and belly respectively represent reason, will and desire. This tripartition of the soul is projected unto the organisation of

Zoroastrian by nature, with every member of the community fulfilling his function, according to the predominance of head (reason, wisdom), heart (courage, passion) or body (appetite). A harmonious state of the whole is ensured if no one tries to interfere in the function of another. The idea of gentle rule through love of learning was also a cornerstone in Plato's writings.

What comes as a true revelation is the passage on learning the highest and noblest truth achieved by individuals who act "rightly and reasonably, in thought, word and deed"[18]. The textual recurrence of the tripartite motto in Plato's writings is essential in confirming that this key to reading our existence forms the basis of Greek ethics. Not only is the act of discernment explicitly present in Plato, as "the universal cause of all rectitude and of all beauty" (*Republic* 517 b), also in *The Laws*, he shows great respect for essential Persian values such as freedom, equality and friendship and admires severe but righteous Persian education[19].

As for Aristotle, we notice a familiar item already present in the *Gathas*. The importance of logic and good reasoning was relentlessly stressed by the great Greek philosophers in their opposition to the fallacious argumentations of the Sophists, who were thoroughly countered by Socrates. In Book IV of his *Ethics*, Aristotle explains how good thinking (*orthos logos*) allows the individual to become wiser and to discover what it means to be good. And in Book X, he addresses the question "whether virtue consists more particularly in the reasoned choice or in the actions". Like Zarathustra, he maintains that it "should satisfy both" and that the true end of actions is not to be found in contemplation or knowledge, but in their execution: "Theoretic science does not suffice; one should also endeavour to possess this virtue" (chapter IX)[20]. The tripartite motto is reaffirmed by Aristotle is his assertion that "we judge of truth (...) from facts and from life" and if our arguments do not agree with facts, "we must consider them as mere words" (chapter VIII).

---

the ideal state divided into rulers, warriors and the people. Each individual occupies the function that best corresponds to them, so that a harmonic state with a good proportion of the different functions will produce the best orderly result.
18 Supplement to the Laws or *Epinomis*, 989 c. He adds: "men will thus be no formal hypocrites but true worshippers of virtue, and this, of course, is the main subject of concern for the whole community".
19 See Book III (693-696), with references to Darius, Cyrus, Cambyses and Xerxes.
20 Aristotle adds: "Of course, if words were sufficient to be virtuous, we should express great gratitude to them".

In his *Metaphysics*, Aristotle defends the idea of the primordial choice, implicitly present in the *Gathas*. He explicitly attributes the idea of good, as the first principle, to the Magi[21]. Interesting in this respect is his critique of Plato's idealism, of goodness being an idea external to a person, as he develops a more dynamic vision of goodness being a quality of the individual who actually develops his potential to become a better person. The difference between the good in act and the good in potency appears to be essential in considering that thinking alone will not be sufficient for a person to be good, just like potentially good is void without the actions. Aristotle's theory of happiness, his eudemonia – literally to have a good demon – implies an equality in potential. Every human has this quality, which he or she can develop for the sake of humanity.

Iran

During more than ten centuries, Mazdeism was the state religion of the Achaemenid Empire and later Iranian regimes (Medes, Parthians and Sasanians) until the invasion of the Arabs in the sixth century AD. The persecutions and forced conversions after the fall of the Sasanian Empire (in 651) did not result in the religion being completely eradicated by the Arab Muslims[22]. The exile to India in the 7th to 9th century ensured that total disappearance was diverted. It cannot be excluded that the assertion of Zoroastrians being monotheists, 'people of the book', with reference to the holy book *Avesta*, dates from that period[23]. From then on, Zoroastrians in Iran practised their religion privately and passed on their ethical way of life from one generation to the next. Today, and in spite of the attempts to ensure the survival of Zoroastrianism, the Islamisation of Iran and the centuries of long and dreadful repression give the impression that Iran was never the 'land of the Aryans'. The figure of Zarathustra is tolerated as a Sufi dating from the so-called pre-Islamic period.

---

21 *Metaphysics* (1091b). Aristotle attributes 'good' as the first principle to some Pre-Socratics, to the Magi, and to later sages such as Empedocles and Anaxagoras.

22 For a history of the Sasanians, see M.R. Jackson Bonner, *Al-Dinawari's 'Kitab al-Akhbar al-Tiwal': An Historiographical Study of Sasanian Iran* (Leuven, Peeters, 2015).

23 In his *Historical and Critical Dictionary* (1697), Pierre Bayle asserts that monotheism was invented in order to survive the Muslim persecutions. Still, it is known that many Zoroastrians in Iran chose to pay the *jizya*, like Jews and Christians, rather than convert to Islam.

An important misconception is that many people think that Iran is part of the Arab world and that the Persian language is the same as Arabic in writing and pronunciation. Or that the Persian and Arab tradition share the same history and culture. As the next section shows, the Persian heritage was appropriated under Muslim rule. But although the Arabs established hegemony over most of Great Iran, the conversion to Islam was never complete, still to this day, with Zoroastrian culture being alive and flourishing[24]. Another misconception, as stated before, is the assimilation of Zoroastrianism with Manicheism, with what was known as the 'church of light'. The founder Mani (Manes in Latin) in the 3rd century AD, carried out a kind of compilation of Zoroastrian, Christian and Gnostic elements, according to one interpretation. Others maintain that he tried to make a synthesis of Buddha, Plato and Jesus.

Mani borrowed some ideas from Zoroastrianism, but he associated the ongoing process to the light with a gradual removal from the world of matter. He adapted existing thoughts to his dualistic doctrine and was responsible for centuries of Manichean interpretation in Europe. This new religion was founded on the dualist doctrine of two reigns, the reign of light and the reign of darkness. These two reigns, in constant combat, were associated with good and evil. Mani maintained that the two reigns were pure originally, but a catastrophic event caused the invasion of light by darkness. In the Manichean worldview, light will reconquer darkness and the physical world will be destroyed. The central motive of progression is that all creation returns back to the light that was once invaded by darkness. If, according to Mani, man is double, this is because his mind and soul (the immortal part) belong to the reign of light and his body (the mortal part) to the reign of darkness. The good soul is in constant combat with the evil body, and wishes to detach itself from anything material while there is life. This way, the body of the deceased can liberate itself from the cycle of incarnations and join the reign of light.

The Zoroastrians did not agree with the idea that Mani transmitted the thinking of Zarathustra, especially because the two reigns were each governed by a master, God and Satan, which gave the impression of two godheads. Zoroastrians priests, who could not accept this heresy, conspired against him. After being incarcerated, Mani was either crucified or died in prison in 274 or 277 AD. King Shapur I, to whom the only work Mani

---

24 See also the chapter on 'Zoroastrians in Islamic Iran', Jenny Rose (2011, pp. 159-188).

ever wrote in Persian was dedicated, was not converted. It is not without interest to know that Shapur I, the king of the Sasanians, was not impressed by Mani, but tolerated him and his followers, and remained Zoroastrian.

The Christians, for their part, also objected to this division of the world in two reigns. How could they accept a reign of light, of divine life, created by God, next to a reign of darkness, the reign of the diabolic, also created by God? The only acceptable explanation was that fallen angels had been expelled from heaven and were led by Satan or the devil, who rebelled against God and seduced humans into falsehood. This is how heaven and hell became two places where the souls go after death, not to be confused with the aforementioned two abodes, the two conditions we find ourselves in according to the tendency we follow. A huge difference occurs when the longing for a paradise in the after-life is replaced by a serene state of mind brought about by having made right choices and when the threat of burning hell is replaced by the actual condition of non-life.

Nevertheless, Mani inspired many followers, and the idea of the victory of the light over darkness spread quickly from the 3rd till the 7th century. It was followed by the Gnostics and adopted by Catharism, a vein of neo-Manicheism that reached Europe. The Cathars rejected the Old Testament and tried to replace Catholicism[25]. Unfortunately, Manichean dualism, with which Zoroastrianism was associated, left its misleading marks on Zoroastrianism, which persist even today.

Persian philosophy

Thanks to the revival of the Silk Road as a focus of travel and study, Persian culture, the cradle of human thought, is beginning to receive more attention. This of course does not alter the fact that historical monuments have systematically been destroyed, archeological sites abandoned and left in ruin. Luckily, not everything is completely lost. I refer to the archeological site of Persepolis and its remains of a great empire, the Achaemenid empire, with its capital Pasargadae and the tomb of Cyrus II, or the 'Cube of

---

25 The Cathars, from *catharos* or pure, interpreted the doctrine of the two reigns as a practice of excessive asceticism and vegetarianism as a return to the pure light. They considered existence as a living hell. They were massacred in France in the 13th century and Catharism in Germany survived until the 14th century.

Zoroaster' in Naqsh-e Rustam, a rectangular building on a triple stair basis. I also refer to the numerous traces of Zoroastrian culture that are conserved in the works of Persian thinkers like Al-Razi, Avicenna, Al-Farabi, Al-Ghazali and Sohrawardi or in the poems of Khayyâm (died in 1131), Rumi (died in 1273), Saadi (died around 1292) and Hafez (died in 1389).

Little known are these texts of a world heritage, including the works that belong to the world history of philosophy. In 2008, an anthology of Persian philosophy was published in London. It bears witness to "the figures of the first schools of Islamic philosophy, who largely influenced the West, and were either Persian and belonged to the Persian territory or underlined the Persian dimension of Islamic civilization"[26]. Outside readers, who are not aware of the political agenda of certain Muslim governments, do not find the use of the term 'pre-Islamic' aberrant. Either it is negatively used to refer to pagan traditions that should be wiped out or in the best case be tolerated, or to anti-Muslim cultures that should be ignored. Silent contempt probably suits Islamic leaders as a most effective strategy to conceal the great Iranian culture that is part of its roots.

Sometimes, even the word Arabic is subtly replaced by the term Islamic, which is contrary to tradition. Arabic philosophy has a long history and originated not in the Arabian Peninsula, but in Baghdad (present-day Iraq). According to the historian of philosophy Al-Farabi (10th century), the library of the Neoplatonic school of Alexandria was transferred to Baghdad. Given the attested competition between the Arab and Persian cultures, mainly during the Persian Abbaside reign[27], the caliphs paid every book that was translated into Arabic in gold, from 750 to 850 AD. Already in the 7th and 8th centuries, Mesopotamians and Syrians had translated the philosophic and scientific treatises coming from the Greek and Roman world into Arabic. But stimulated by the Abbasid caliphs in Baghdad, thinkers like Al-Kindi contributed to the translations in Arabic of the dialogues of Plato and the complete works of Aristotle. This 9th century philosopher is sometimes designated as the father of Arab philosophy.

---

26 Seyyed Hossein Nasr and Mehdi Aminrazavi, *An Anthology of Philosophy in Persia: Zoroaster to Umar Khayyam* (Vol I, London-New York, Tauris, 2008, pp.1-4).

27 Most impressive is the work of Jacqueline Chabbi, *Le Seigneur des tribus. L'islam de Mahomet* (Paris, CNRS, 2010). The author tries to reconstruct the history of the first caliphates, on the basis of the work of the Iranian Tabari (10th century).

So, a substantial part of Greek antiquity was available in Iran in the 9th century. The Abbasids considered themselves as the legitimate inheritors of Greek Antiquity (instead of the Byzantines whom they saw as their rivals). Religion did not play a prominent role in the development of the discussed subjects, as it didn't all through the golden age of Islam that ended with Averroes at the end of the twelfth century. The Arabic tradition mainly combined Aristotelianism with Neoplatonist ideas and so doing, discretely sowed the seeds of Zoroastrian thinking. For numerous Persian scientists and poets, the only way to guarantee the survival of Persian Antiquity under Muslim or Islamic rule, was to not openly admit they were indebted to Zoroastrian thinking. Nevertheless, they could tacitly praise him in their works; they could indirectly refer to their great past in a hidden way and celebrate the joys of music, wine, and of being free and responsible men and women, keen to be the guardians of the process to completion.

Again, there is no reason to erroneously repeat that there is no such thing as Persian philosophy. Even if it was integrated in the history of Arabic thinking under the label of pre-Islamic culture, it should not be subordinated to Islamic theology. Eventually, special attention could be devoted to the identifiable Zoroastrian elements in Muslim religion or in pan-Arabic culture. For instance, there is the daily jihad against falseness, namely the inner battle between two opposite tendencies. During prayer, the faithful observes which of the two takes the upper hand while addressing the confidant inside. Muslims, like Zoroastrians, say prayer five times a day, with this difference that the former are turned towards Makkah, invariably taking the east as a point of reference, while Zoroastrians follow the position of the sun during its daily journey across the sky and trust the night to bring a new dynamics[28]. Also, the Persian heritage is kept alive thanks to the use of the name *Khoda*, the Indo-European root of God, rather than the Arabic *Allah*, also defined in terms of light: "Allah is the light of the heavens and the earth".

---

28 A brief reference is made here to Mithraism and the symbol of the solar revolution in the form of a cross in a circle. The four points of the cross represented the different stadia of the sun. In Christianity, the cross became a symbol of suffering and redemption, but the importance of the solar symbolism remained. Let us be reminded that Mithraism was the official religion in Rome during more than three centuries. Mithraeums were built throughout Europe until the 4th century AD, the remains of which can still be found along the rivers Danube and the Rhine, and as far as in England and Spain.

Part Four. Where? 131

Neoplatonist renaissance and Sufism

From the eleventh century on, Persian Neoplatonism was an important school of thought for many Muslim writers who revived the flame of ancient Persian wisdom. In different ways, Zarathustra's universal message was resurrected, and this was still the case until recently, with writers like Tagore and Gibran perpetuating the tradition[29]. A new element in the discussion was an issue that can be summarized as follows: the Persian Neoplatonists considered that religions could be replaced by a religious Neoplatonism. The Neoplatonist school of Athens (Iamblicus, Proclus) sought to follow the traditional rites in a religious way, while Neoplatonists like Plotinus and his disciple Porphyry considered religious practice as undignified for sages.

In the 3rd century AD, Plotinus – who had studied in Alexandria, where oriental spiritualism flourished – relied on Philon (and his universalist vision). Plotinus travelled later to Persia and India, where he was directly immersed into local practices[30]. His later influence on Persian Neoplatonism and Sufi mysticism was huge, considering that his theory of emanation and the light metaphor were propagated during centuries in Eastern and Western Neoplatonism. He was clearly on the same wavelength as Zarathustra. Medieval Persian thinkers like Farabi, Avicenna or Sohrawardi, were much indebted to the theories of Plotinus. His texts, together with the works of Plato, were translated in Italy, at the Academy of Florence, influencing Italian Renaissance.

The competition between theory and practice gained ground in medieval Persia, partly because of the interaction with the Neoplatonism of Rome and Athens. For instance, the heritage from Greek and Roman antiquity caused discussions about how Plato and Aristotle could be categorised. The question was raised whether Aristotle was a logician and Plato a theologian.

---

29   Rabindranath Tagore (1861-1941), Nobel Prize of Literature in 1913, gave many conferences on Zarathustra in India (published in *The Religion of Man*, 1931). And the Lebanese author Khalil Gibran (1883-1931), who was inspired by Nietzsche, is the author of *The prophet*, one of the world's best-selling books after Shakespeare and Lao-Tse.

30   Porphyre describes in the *Life of Plotinus* that his master tried to gain direct knowledge of Persian and Indian practices. The orientalism of Plotinus can be summarized as pertaining to two elements, the metaphor of light and the concept of One (he found his inspiration in the Indian concept of *advaïta* (not-twoness and in post-Zoroastrian Mazdeism).

A separation seemed necessary between mysticism, considered too spiritual, and Neoplatonism, considered too cerebral. By the time the opposition of religious practice and philosophic theory in Neoplatonist renaissance became overriding, the symbiotic character of the 'eyes of the heart' was not so self-evident. The eyes and the heart started to follow two distinct ways.

From the 8th century onward, Sufism had served as a kind of cement connecting philosophical practices (mystical experiences, theosophy of light) and theoretical philosophical thinking (oriental Neoplatonism). What is mostly ignored is the role played by the first Sufis like Rabi'a al-Adawija or Rabi of Basra (713-801) and by Al-Hallaj, who in the tenth century was hanged in the public square because of heresy, for having described his relation to God in delirious ecstasy. Certain Sufis, like Sohrawardi, followed a theosophy of light and seemed to renew the proposition of Zarathustra to base one's life on the eyes and the heart[31]. More well-known is Rumi, who emigrated to Turkey (during the Mongol invasion) and succeeded in building bridges between theosophy and rationalism.

Although the Neoplatonist thinkers wrote in Arabic, Avicenna was the first philosopher who, in the eleventh century, decided to write in Persian. He wanted to return to the origin of philosophy, to the place where the light came to be. Thinkers like Avicenna were not always able to explicitly comment on the source of oriental thinking, but still found ways of indirectly keeping alive elements of Zoroastrian interest. To be noticed is the syncretism that survived in the light metaphor and in the theory passed down through the ages of one source from which everything emanated. Persian Neoplatonism underlined the idea of emanation, of degrees of light coming from a source illuminating the human mind and soul. This sensitivity for the play of light and shadow can be noticed in the different fields of architecture, tapestry, pottery and poetry.

Spain

In the 7th century, Isidor, bishop of Seville, composed 25 books of etymological analysis, including a section entitled *De Magis*[32]. He was

---

[31] Karen Armstrong establishes interesting links between Neoplatonism and Zoroastrianism. *A History of God. The 4000-Year Quest of Judaism, Christianity and Islam* (New York, Ballantine, 1994).

[32] The text on the Magi can be found in *Etymologies,* Book VIII.

seeking to transmit a body of knowledge threatened with disappearance. His work, based on the explanation of names and keywords in ancient wisdom, remained famous until the Renaissance. Isidor mentioned the name of Zarathustra and declared that the Magi practised astrology and divination (by observing the flight of birds, lightning, the constellation of stars). He did not conceal the existence of deceitful Magi who travelled around the world during centuries, with an ability to mislead people by foretelling the future, invoking the dead or imploring malicious angels.

With regard to Zarathustra, Isidor mentions him as the first magician (sic), king of Bactria, who was killed in a battle with the king of the Assyrians. He claims that Aristotle attributed the composition of two million verses to Zarathustra. And that Democritus contributed in the spreading of his knowledge during many centuries. It is in fact known that the Persian king Xerxes personally paid a visit to the atomist Democritus. This way, the idea of a direct line of thought persisted in 7th century Europe. And even earlier, considering that the Church Father Augustin (5th century), for instance, was aware of the importance of the Zoroastrian way of life. It was through the Manichean doctrine (before converting to Christianity) that Augustin knew of Zoroastrian ideas. He shared this opinion that the prophet deserved a new status instead of being denigrated as a diviner or magician.

In Muslim Spain of the 11th century, there was an important translation centre. More specifically in Andalusia where the three world monotheisms seem to have coexisted peacefully. It is during that period that the Europeans were informed of the existence of the works of the great Greek philosophers in Arabic. We cannot overstress the importance of the fact that the West ultimately had access to the content of numerous works of Greek philosophy. The Toledo School of Translators was a multilingual centre where during four centuries the classical works of Greek thinkers were translated, mainly from classic Arabic into Latin, but also into Hebrew. Also in Toledo, governed by the Muslims from 711 and reconquered by the Christians in 1085, the works of Persian thinkers like Farabi, Avicenna and Ghazali were translated in the 12th century[33].

---

33 For the 'jihad of the philosophers', such as Avicenna and Averroes, I refer to Remi Brague, *Au moyen du Moyen-Âge. Philosophies médiévales en chrétienté, judaïsme et islam* (Chatou, La Transparence, 2006).

Andalusia gained celebrity thanks to thinkers like Ibn Arabi and Averroes (12th century). Thomas Aquinas (13th century) would not have written his *Ente et essentia* without the translations of Avicenna and Averroes, against whom he polemicised over the immortality of the individual soul. A whole new question arose that concerned the way humans should relate to the light and on whether the light of wisdom can be propagated to everyone. Ibn Arabi defended restricting to the ignorant the information concerning the different ways of approaching the light, while not depriving those who are in the position to receive it and who deserve to receive it. Averroes agreed that not all individuals are ready to receive the light, because it could also harm them, and so he invented the theory of the 'double truth'[34].

To favour tempered light and to recommend veiled transmission was quite unusual in the West, including the idea that darkness is not unilaterally bad. Seen from a specific perspective, darkness gives birth to light and is to be valued as such. The night gives strength to the day, both night and day depending on each other and both invariably following each other. The moon with its capacity to regularly change its shape and disappear for days on end is more dynamic than the sun, which explains why the moon is a powerful symbol in Arabic cultures. As mentioned before, the changing intensity of moonlight is attested in this Gathic verse: "Who made the moon to sometimes wax and sometimes wane?" (44,3); and the changing position of the planets: "What being laid down paths for the sun and the stars?" (44,3). The sensitivity for a dynamic vision of light-sources indeed sharpens the sensitivity of humans for the well-ordered cosmic regulation and may stimulate praise. The act of praising can be life-giving and is one of the ways of reviving cosmic dynamism and taking part in it.

Italian Renaissance

There was a very strong link between Oriental and Italian renaissance, and Zarathustra's world view constituted a great source of inspiration. The *re*-naissance, that is the power to be re-born, was not just a concept; it was the driving source behind the connecting element between the East

---

34 According to Averroes, simple souls will understand the metaphor of God as light literally as we see the sun, while the learned will know that God's beatitude is increasing wisdom. These two categories of truth refer to the intellect of individuals, to the way one relates, respectively to relative or to absolute wisdom.

and the West. In the heat of the Italian Renaissance, the filiation between Zarathustra and Plato was reconfirmed. Universalist ideas permeated European universities and academies, turning Zarathustra into the "founder of the seven liberal arts", according to a 15th century image, conserved in the British Library (collection Cotton Augustus).

Thirty centuries separated oriental wisdom from its rebirth in Italy, with a noticeable transition from the concept of the static and pure essence of light to a dynamic vision that was explicitly promoted. The emphasis on perspective in the fine arts and the interactive relation to light is indeed just one parameter to approach the continuum of intellectual knowledge connecting East and West. This was already a fact during the Abbasside reign in the 8th and 9th centuries, but the Persian spark was soon to be re-ignited by the Byzantine philosopher Georgius Gemistus Pletho (14th-15th century). We tend in fact to forget that the renewed interest in Zarathustra of the Neoplatonist Ficino was due to Pletho, responsible of the Zoroastrian revival[35].

At the Academy of Florence, Ficino worked together with Pletho, who published works in which he insisted on the direct filiation between Zarathustra and Plato. Pletho was influenced by the Sufi Sohrawardi and developed the theory of "the golden chain" which started with Zarathustra, the first great thinker. He argued that a universal philosophy existed long before Christianity and that a re-hellinisation and a re-paganisation could restore the splendour of Greek Antiquity. Pletho founded his philosophy on Zarathustra, on the theory of freedom as responsibility. But after accusations of scandal in his classes on Plato, he was arrested for heresy and exiled to Mistra, in the heart of the Peloponnese, to a study centre where he met Byzantine intellectuals.

Now, Pletho defended Greek philosophy against the Christian doctrine whose weak spot was faith instead of the force that stems from the practices of virtue. He did not want religions to disappear, but was convinced they could be replaced by a Neoplatonic religion close to a theosophy of light. Above all, he was a cosmopolite, having studied in Constantinople with Jews, Christians and Muslims. Probably because of his reputation, Pletho

---

35 Henry Corbin observed that Pletho was directly influenced by Sohrawardi. See *Inside Iranian Islam*, Vol. 2. And Pletho first heard of Zarathustra in his contact with a Hebrew sufi Elisha, an erring Israqi. For a more exhaustive study on Pletho, I refer to the excellent introduction by Moreno Neri to his translation of the Treatise on Virtue (Pletone, *Trattato delle virtù*, Milano, Bompiani, 2010).

was called to Florence, at the court of the Medici, to arbitrate the unification of the Roman Church, where he founded a new Neoplatonist school, based on "the most ancient sage whose name reached us". It was thanks to Pletho that Zarathustra was redefined as the Persian sage who inspired Plato[36].

In 15th century Italy, Pico della Mirandola had advanced the idea of free will and of freedom as the foundation of human dignity. Pico claimed that he possessed a manuscript with secret Chaldean texts and declared that it was "Zoroaster, according to the writings of Chaldean interpreters, who qualified the soul as being 'winged' ". He argued that the intermediary position of man which incited to study nature, all of nature, and his inner universe, was first described by Zarathustra and then by Plato. As did Plato, he presented Zarathustra as a "son of Oromase" and maintained that the Persian sage had preceded the Holy Scriptures and the Greek philosophers. He could only recommend his listeners: "be attentive, Fathers, to the teachings of Zoroaster, and consider their meaning with care"[37].

Marcilio Ficino, who met Pico in 1486, also drew upon Zarathustra. Together with the Platonists of his time, he insisted on what was called "the return to light" according to the different levels of the person that receives it. To return to the light and join Oneness was compared to a movement upstream, towards the source where the light comes from. Actually, the Persian Neoplatonists physically experienced divine light, which infinitely spreads and rises up in man when he exposes himself to it. The indispensable condition for joining God is indispensable openness so that the soul may let in the light, which transforms itself in living energy. Eloquence did not take precedence in Persian Neoplatonism, but the reintegration of the individual into divine light and the unification with intelligibility, with the One. Not reasoning, but the mystical dimension was overriding, the effective union, the reunion with Oneness.

England

In 17th century Europe, Manicheism and Catharism were considered heresies in the eyes of the official Church of Rome and the Anglican Church.

---

36 Pletho died in Mistra, but the remains of his body were brought to Rimini where Sigismondo Malatesta interred them in a sarcophagus in the Malatesta Temple.
37 http://www.lyber-eclat.net/lyber/mirandola/pico.html

In a climate where churches were violently trying not to lose control, the English orientalist, Thomas Hyde, professor at the University of Oxford, made a monumental compilation of all the elements that were known about Persian and pre-Islamic religions in Iran[38]. He did not particularly praise the quality of Persian thinking, but he was most certainly a forerunner in the comparative study of religions. Hyde elevated Zarathustra to the rank of prophets who received the monotheistic revelation. In doing so, he based himself on a pseudo-biography according to which the Persian sage was the server of a Jewish prophet who had been able to transfer his knowledge all the way to Iran.

This Jewish aspect enabled Hyde to raise an important question concerning Christian theology. If the Persian prophet was able to fathom the mystery of revelation and announce the coming of the Messiah, he was decidedly no heretic and the accusation that Zoroastrianism was a heretic dualist doctrine no longer held up in 17th century Christianity. Hyde presented Zarathustra not as a Manichean dualist, but as a real reformer. As a result, the West needed to concede that he played an important role in the history of humanity. Hyde's contribution in the restoration of the figure of Zarathustra was considerable, but there is little doubt today that Hyde placed the Persian prophet in the firing line of the Protestants in their opposition against the Catholics.

After Hyde's historical study, the philosopher David Hume published his *Natural History of Religion* in 1757. He relied on the information available at the time; on the information coming from the reports of the first travellers. The fascination for the Iranian and Indian 'Guebres' had everything to do with what was perceived as an affinity with Christian elements[39]. All the same, Hume observed that the Magi were sectarian and that the disciples of Zarathustra had closed the doors of paradise to other populations. He valued the fact that they had rejected idolatry and referred to an 'original intelligence' as the principle of all things. Furthermore, he remarked that this original intelligence "manifests itself immediately to good understanding". He did however equate this intelligence with the physical sun, in a dualist logic of the visible world as a copy of the

---

38 Thomas Hyde, *The History of the religion of ancient Persia* (1700).
39 Jenny Rose associates the word 'guèbre' or 'gaur', with new Persian 'gabr'. The Safavids used the word 'gabr-mahalle' to designate the Zoroastrian quarter outside the city wall of Kerman. 17th century European travelers gave the name Gabrestan for the Zoroastrian section of Isfahan (Jenny Rose, 176).

invisible world. Hume, then, followed mainstream opinion in the West that stubbornly identified physical light and wisdom in the East, and misjudged the fire and light symbolism[40].

Hélène Blavatsky was a pioneer in vigorously rejecting these presuppositions. She stood up against the erroneous vision that the pagans worship the sun itself, rather than the creator of the sun. She also underlined that the Egyptians worshiped the sun, but that the sun was the eye of Osiris, not Osiris himself. As the founder of theosophy, Blavatsky encouraged the comparative study of religions, philosophy and science, and after an encounter with American freemasons, she founded the Theosophical Society in New York (1875). Its major objective was to contribute to a better knowledge of Zarathustra and to enhance the idea of a universal fraternity of humanity. In Chennai, India, one can still visit the Centre of Research and the garden with replicas of the temples of the main world religions; there is also a central building regrouping the representatives of the different schools of thought, among which Zarathustra Spitama.

The Orient as the homeland of the new light shining on the Western world renewed the interest in mystery cults, in Hermetism, Mithraicism, Phrygianism, Orphism, Isis cults and esotery in general. From the 18th century onwards, the birth of orientalism was perceived as a return to paganism[41]. Freemasonry, officially founded in 1717, welcomed secret knowledge, and the creation of lodges as platforms of encounter was key to building a humane society the world over. The idea of uniting men (!) of all nations was based on universal fraternity and on an eclectic number of references to ancient cults. Chevalier Ramsay, who published *Voyages de Cyrus* in 1727 even defended the idea of a universal religion. Ramsay praised the Persians who still possess "the sublime science of being happy with simple nature". Persian symbolism functioned as an important tool in

---

40 Hume concluded that Zoroastrian religion would never be able to become a universal religion – a lively issue in the 18th century. Once again, we see that the comparative study of religions inevitably produces interpretations depending on one's own religion and culture. *The philosophical works of David Hume* (Vol 7, Edinburgh, Black and Tait, 1826, pp. 469ff).

41 At the end of the 18th century, it would give rise to English romanticism, with its emphasis on emotion and the glorification of the past and nature. And German romanticism was so much impressed by the ingenuity of nature, by the assimilation of the creator with the genius of nature, that it created a pantheist atmosphere and a return to paganism. The cosmos is divinely inspired which has brought about the celebration of an ineffable God, without representation or name.

Freemasonry. A Scottish banner of the 18th century features the instruction "bien penser, bien parler, bien agir"[42].

France

In England, France and Germany there appeared a current of freethinkers and Zarathustra was welcomed as a great reformer. In the Age of Enlightenment, more precisely from 1670 onwards, the figure of the freethinker was associated with an enlightened deism, against the tyranny of the church. In those days, an eclectic choice of texts on the 'thoughts of Zoroaster' circulated and generated a multitude of reflections. A whole new era seemed to arise based on the idea that the best times were yet to come. This new perspective on the future, founded on the equality of man liberated a creative energy in favour of individual development and education, which became a right. If the enlightened mind of every individual is made to count, then the universe will evolve in the good direction, was the leading idea.

Reflective judgement was promoted as a good instrument in the evolution towards universal comprehension. Its implication was the emancipation from power hungry leaders and the promotion of (ancient Persian) values such as freedom, equality and friendship. Too few realise that these principles were written down about 32 centuries before The Declaration of Human Rights (1789). The Cyrus Cylinder dan indeed be regarded as the oldest charter on human liberty, written in cuneiform script on a clay cylinder. It includes the idea of freedom of religion and tolerance towards other cultures. It is preserved in the British Museum, and on the internet one can read the complete declaration by the Persian king Cyrus the Great (6th century BC) who states that all men (the people of Babylon, Sumer and Akkad) are free to worship their own gods and that no one should be mistreated for this. That individuals should be respectful to one another so that peace and tranquillity can be guaranteed. And that everyone can live in peace in the country of his choice[43].

---

42   Ramsay believed that Christian freemasonry was best placed to found a unified religion. Freemasons hold introspection to be a good way of preserving rectitude and integrity, and working towards the completion of humanity. The name of Zarathustra designates a superior degree of masons.

43   For the most up-to-date translation of the Akkadian text, see: https://www.britishmuseum.org/research/collection_online/collection_object_details.aspx?objectId=327188&partId=1

Eighteenth-century French thinkers, advocating for emancipation from leaders who rejected the idea that communities are bound by reason rather than by religious dogmas, turned Zarathustra into an ally against the clergy. The argument was that if Judeo-Christianism was not the only religion, then Zoroaster could bring an alternative, especially since he could be seen as championing the fight against hypocrisy. So, on the threshold of the age of enlightenment, the new information from the Orient aroused a great deal of interest among Western scholars. The side-effect of this interest in orientalism was a growing fascination for pagan cultures, not only those of Rome and Egypt, but also those of the Middle and Far East. If the pagan and Christian doctrines really did feature significant similarities, then what was at stake was a revision of the monopoly of Jews and Christians on monotheism.

In 1697, Pierre Bayle rehabilitated Zarathustra who was presented as a victim of falsifications and prejudices. In his *Historical and Critical Dictionary*, Bayle stated that we have no knowledge of the history of Zarathustra and he presented a fictionalized Zoroaster. He discredited the traditional sources as being contradictory and alternatively depicted an excellent prophet, who deserved to be praised for having distinguished good from bad. Bayle would not be the only scholar during the Age of Enlightenment to consider Zarathustra as figure of authority and moral. In sum, Zarathustra emerged as a hero from the discourse of the Enlightenment.

This was mainly due to Voltaire who had been impressed by the translations of Anquetil-Duperron. In his *Dictionary of Philosophy*, Zoroaster is presented as the founder of a great religion in Iran. Voltaire, who of course could only rely on the information that was available at the time, mainly targeted men of power. His interest in Zarathustra was fuelled by the idea that Moses did not have a monopoly on monotheism and he could find in Hyde the arguments he needed to combat the Catholic Church. Whereas Zarathustra denounced hypocrisy in all men and women, this foreign "enlightened deist" suited Voltaire's purpose as a weapon in the struggle for the freedom to think for oneself against dogmatic doctrines.

As from 1751, Voltaire published texts that aimed at a broader audience[44]. This body of practical philosophy commented on themes such as the lie,

---

44 Section 39 in *Le Philosophe ignorant* (Paris, Flammarion, 2009) is on Zarathustra. It was Voltaire who attributed this quotation to Zarathustra: "When you are in

the ruse, deceitful eloquence, sincerity, blindness, ignorance. It was an interesting choice of themes. Voltaire claimed that philosophy is alive only when it is able to influence the conduct of people. He found inspiration in the philosophy of Zarathustra, of which he appreciated the pragmatic aspect. Forms of behaviour such as idleness, laziness and cowardice attracted the attention of thinkers like Voltaire, but also Kant, who read a translation of the *Gathas* in German. Voltaire ended his book *Candide* with the words: "We must cultivate our garden", whereby the reader is invited to make the effort to discover the truth within and to engage in self-understanding; to grow and to nourish one's potential to progress and not to allow events to take over.

Germany

The metaphor of light captured the attention of philosophers, poets and musicians during the European revival of Zoroastrian thinking. The idea of universal brotherhood inspired Schiller and Beethoven, and in Mozart's *Magic Flute*, Sarastro is a sage who encourages the passage from the reign of night to the reign of day. Already in 1733, Zoroaster was a wise hero in Handel's *Orlando* and in 1749 Rameau wrote an opera on Zarathustra. Most famous is *Also sprach Zarathustra* by Richard Strauss (1896), inspired by Nietzsche's book[45]. In German romanticism, Zarathustra was resurrected in the philosophical works of Herder, Lessing and Hegel and in poetry, with authors like Von Kleist and his *Prayer of Zoroaster* (1810)[46].

Before then, in the eighteenth century, in his call for us to think (*sapere aude*, the maxim of Horatius), the philosopher Immanuel Kant discovered a form of enlightened universalism in Zarathustra and he encouraged the development of critical thinking. He knew about the Zoroastrian way of

---

doubt abstain".
45 To be noted is also *A Mass of Life* by Frederick Delius or the 'Midnight Song' (*Symphony No 3*) by Gustav Mahler. But it is the Belgian composer Janpieter Biesemans, who for the first time put 13 verses of the *Gathas* (2012) to music, who deserves to be especially praised. The musical theme of Strauss was used by Stanley Kubrick for the spatial aurora in *A Space Odyssey* (1968). The Brazilian group Deodato produced a jazz-rock version of the theme. Elvis Presley's stage appearance in a world-wide television broadcast was accompanied by the theme; and the group Deep Purple used it to open their concert *Live in Geneva*.
46 I also refer to Shelley, who evokes a meeting with Zoroaster and his soul in *Prometheus Unbound* (1820).

life and was interested in ideas that seem "inherent to all human reason"[47]. One hundred years after Spinoza, and one hundred years before Nietzsche, Kant turned to universal imperatives and developed a kind of morals of work. Through laziness and cowardice, mankind turns away from its responsibilities, observed Kant. Instead of burdening others with one's own existential work, each person should develop a moral regeneration.

Kant was so impressed by the figure of Zarathustra that in 1802 he considered inserting his name in the title of his book on religion[48]. This is not surprising, considering that we recognise in his maxims and categorical imperatives the necessity of the primordial choice and of universal imperatives that should be in harmony with practical reason. Kant specified that what you ought to do is to act according to the logic of a universal law. He observed that moral autonomy is not sufficient if each rational being does not also endorse the principle himself[49]. It is not enough to expect others to adopt the right conduct; one should also place high demands on oneself. Instead of burdening others with unpleasant tasks, one develops the free will that operates in accordance with universal self-imposed laws. More precisely, freedom of choice can be determined only if maxims can assume the form of universal laws and if each subject feels duty-bound by maxims that could be universally self-legislated.

Hegel, for his part, maintained that philosophy originated in the West, but admitted "the spirit was born in the East"[50]. In Hegelian philosophy, the evolution of humanity is formulated in terms of a progression, toward

---

47 Kant knew of the first German translation of the *Gathas* (from the French edition of Anquetil-Duperron) by Johann Friedrich Kleuker in 1776.
48 The translator of Kant's first Critique, Norman Kemp Smith, *A Commentary to Kant's Critique of Pure Reason*, refers to the two titles Kant considered by (Palgrave, McMillan, 2nd ed., 2003, p. 610). Eckart Förster published an essay on the posthumous work of Kant and observed that Zarathustra appeared to Kant as an archetypical figure, the ideal of theoretical reason and practical reason unified in the human who is consistent with moral duty (*Kant's Final Synthesis*, Cambridge, University Press, 19989, p. 284).
49 In his *Religion within the Boundaries of Mere Reason* (1793-94), Kant dedicates the third part to "the victory of good over evil" and to "establishing a reign of God on earth". He declares that the "Parsis, who subscribe to the religion of Zoroaster, have preserved their faith up till the present day despite their dispersion, because their high priests possessed the Zendavesta, the holy book of their faith".
50 *Vorlesungen über die Geschichte der Philosophie* (Vol I, Frankfurt, Suhrkamp, 1971, p. 120-121).

universal light. Hegel dedicated a whole chapter of his aesthetics to the religion of Zoroaster and declared that the first sensible representation of the absolute has been accomplished in the light that came into being in the East with the religion of Zoroaster, in Ancient Persia[51]. According to Hegel, the conflict between light and darkness is determinant for a perpetual movement towards the light. And he maintained that humans are related to the light, to goodness, as something objective and confirmed by their will[52]. Although he conceded that the mind arises in the East, he added that India and China have no morals, no legislation and that nothing is determined, because everything is founded on the aleatory character of the order of nature.

Hegel developed his phenomenology of natural religion on the basis of the conflict of light and darkness which guarantees a perpetual movement. As he was familiar with the Zoroastrian vision, it is not excluded that his dialectics found its inspiration in his reading of oriental texts. Indeed, in his aesthetics of light, Hegel shows how the individual mind (or spirit), aware of itself, becomes absolute mind (or spirit) and annihilates its internal contradictions. His theory of light describes a movement of invisible light, determining itself by its incarnation in the world and encountering the conflict with the obscure, with a material object. In a dialectic process, it encounters obscurity and must free itself from impurities. In Hegel's approach, the impure should be eradicated, so that pure light, and it alone, may subsist. Indeed, Hegelian dialectic dualism reflects the direction towards infinite light, the search of unity, towards the mind (or spirit) finally becoming absolute, in an ever-recurrent movement until the end of history.

Hegel was under the impression that the Parsis in India made Ormuzd prevail in their thinking. These "beings of light" keep dark thoughts at a distance, he observed, so that the purity of light can propagate without too many obstacles. According to him, this religion based on natural phenomena entails a particular moral: people who are oriented towards the light, also spread the light unto others[53]. And he was impressed by the conflict between Ormuzd and Ahriman, which he considered to be without resolve, and regretted that Ormuzd is inseparable from its sensible existence as light. This

---

51   *Ästhetik* (Vol I, Frankfurt, Europäische Verlagsanstalt, 1955, pp. 319-322).
52   *Vorlesungen* über *die Philosophie der Geschichte* contains chapters on Zarathustra, the Persians and the Zend-people (Frankfurt, Suhrkamp, 1970, pp. 215-236).
53   Hegel was impressed by the reign of light and knew about the 'Ameshaspands'. See the chapter on 'philosophy of good or of light' in *Vorlesungen* über *die Philosophie der Religion* (Frankfurt, Suhrkamp, 1969, pp. 395-406).

brought him to the conclusion that absolute conscience of self is absent, thus allocating superiority to the Christian God, who is spiritual and personal.

India

Till this day, a fire is kept burning in Zoroastrian temples (known as *atash Bahram* or *agiary*, depending on the grade of fire) in India. Not so in Iran, with the exception of the fire temple of Yazd, which is said to contain a sacred fire that has been burning for 1500 years, with priests keeping it alive day and night. By the tenth century, practically all the fire temples in Iran were destroyed, but they rose anew in India. The *Zartoshtis* who migrated to India during the Arab invasion of the 7th century in Iran, were given refuge in Gujarat. This exile took place until the 10th century. The migration to India brought about new communities, also called Parsi or Parsi colonies. These communities had to protect themselves and isolation seemed to be the best way of preserving the Zoroastrian heritage.

If little is known about the exact periodisation of prohibitions, customs, worship and ceremonies, several studies were published on Zoroastrian ritual practice[54]. Central agents are water and fire and man's responsibility to keep them clean and pure, even though they should not one-sidedly be interpreted as purification rites[55]. As to the question of vegetarianism, the *Gathas* do not enable us to identify anything of the kind. The Greek

---

54 Apart from the studies already mentioned, I refer to Jacques Duchesne-Guillemin, *The Western Response to Zoroaster* (Oxford, Clarendon, 1958); Mary Boyce, *Zoroastrians: Their Religious Beliefs and Practices* (London-Boston-Henley, Routledge & Kegan, 1979); Jean Varenne, *Zoroastre: le prophète de l'Iran* (Paris, Dervy, 2012); and more recently, Antonio Panaino, *Zoroastrismo: Storia, temi, attualità* (Brescia, Morcelliana, 2016).

55 This is only one example that shows that purifying and cleansing techniques have their function in ritual practice, but that another aspect can also be suggested. With regard to the exposure of dead bodies to the sun (a *Vendidad* prescription), the emphasis is often on the prevention of contamination of water, earth and fire by the disposal, burial or burning of the dead body. Still, one can also point to the beautiful use of allowing birds of prey to consume the flesh, leaving nothing but the bones within two hours, then letting the sun and the air completely bleach the bones within a few days. Once crumbled to dust, they are washed by the rain and run into the central pit where the bone dust is filtered and ultimately reaches the soil. The flesh and the blood do not directly contaminate the water. Can we not commend this cyclical process and the near absence of human intervention in committing dead bodies to the elements?

historians explained that it was contacts between Pythagoras and the Zoroastrianised Magi in Babylon that inspired the Pythagoreans to adopt a vegetarian and ascetic way of life. Now, Zarathustra might have advised his listeners not to kill animals because the world of plants is rich enough to feed and clothe (Zoroastrians wore white linen), so vegetarianism must have been more than a disciplinary choice. To sacrifice innocent animals for the sole profit of spiritual well-being may have been perceived as a senseless and unnecessary act[56].

We must remember that in remoted times, there were no temples, no places of worship and no liturgical offices. The first communities reunited in the open, under the starry sky, in respectful relationship with all things. The fire they lit radiated like a universal form of solidarity, in their midst, and for the good of all. As soon as the mago-zoroastrians were able to rely on a clergy, specific rituals were institutionalised. In spite of the Zoroastrian exile and diaspora, numerous rituals and customs could fortunately be saved. The transportation of sacred texts overseas from Iran to India and of the sacred fire that survived the journey, ensured that an important part of the tradition was preserved. Ever since, the Parsis in India have protected the inner rituals, the initiation rite and death ceremonies[57], although Hindu elements were able to infiltrate the Parsi cult, which gave rise to a difference between the Zoroastrianism of Parsis and that of Iranian Zoroastrians. Luckily, idolatry has been warded off and reduced to a minimum, as was the wish of Zarathustra.

Perhaps the main difference between Hindus and Zoroastrians is that in Hinduism, the ultimate detachment of the soul from the body and the passage to an afterlife is linked to the doctrine of reincarnation. According to the Parsi scholar Irach J.S. Taraporewalla, there is no condemnation or reward in the *Gathas*, no learning from faults or lessons to be taught[58]. Taraporewalla stresses the impossibility of returning to a worldly existence

---

56   Vegetarianism can be considered a logical result of protection, but it was never forbidden to consume animal products. Only in some derived currents is strict vegetarian consumption promoted. Jacques Duchesne-Guillemin highlights a major change introduced by Zarathustra who rejected Mithra and bloody sacrifice (*Les Religions de l'Orient ancient,* Étienne Drioton, Georges Contenau, J. Duchesne-Guillemin, Paris, Fayard, 1957, p. 106).
57   *Days of Transition* by Dorothea Lüdeckens & Ramiyar Karanjia is a study on death and mourning (Göttingen, Wallstein, 2011).
58   Taraporewalla (1979), p. 32 and p. 35 for the following quotes.

after death, of being given a second chance to lead a better life; this life provides the only chance of living to the full. A repeated return to a worldly existence in accordance with the law of karma is completely different from a progressive evolution until completion.

Taraporewalla underlines that Zoroastrianism is a 'religion of action', of 'right action' and maintains that Zarathustra laid special emphasis upon the inner action and upon helping the needy. He devotes special attention to the hymn *ahuna-vaiira* and mentions the importance of work to Zoroastrians. "We are to *work* all our lives and work in the right manner", he claims. The girdle round the waist, or *kusti*, worn daily by Zoroastrians, is tied three times around the waist with four knots, two in the front and two behind. The actual tying coincides with the word 'working', reminding that we are workers, says Taraporewalla: "our life is not for mere contemplation and dreaming about good, but in active pursuit of good and also in active fighting against evil". And he adds that consciously lighting the fire is a ritual reflecting the taking on of an initiative, so that it does not burn too fast or consume too quickly, placing it under the control of attention and prudence.

Neo-Zoroastrianism

In 2007, Michael Stausberg proposed the term 'para-Zoroastrianism' to designate the new phenomenon of Zoroastrians who do not originate from the official communities of the religion[59]. He regrets the "mimetic heritage" of the new Zoroastrians in Russia, Tadjikistan, Uzbekistan, Kurdistan or Turkmenistan. These para-Zoroastrians are looking for no more than an alternative to Islam, he states. They escape into a religion of which they only know the exterior elements. The worldwide diaspora, especially since the revolution in Iran in 1979, has brought about new contacts and collaborations with non-Zoroastrians and favoured intermarriages with non-Zoroastrians, which according to Stausberg, has caused a "modern reconfiguration".

Apart from these considerations, it appears that the majority of Zoroastrians in the United States, Australia, India, China and Europe, has an ethnic Iranian or Parsi provenance. They have committed to a way of life that is not necessarily governed by an organised religion. They are engaged

---

59   Michael Stausberg, *Faszination Zarathushtra. Zoroaster und die europäische Religionsgeschichte der Frühen Neuzeit* (Berlin-New York, De Gruyter, 1998).

in a cultural substrate and hope to live a decent life in which freedom of choice is based on rectitude and loyalty. There are others who are eager to observe the tradition including the idea of not allowing conversion[60]. They believe that the training of priests is of crucial importance if Zoroastrianism is to remain a world religion. Some of them may also feel that people do not always turn to Zoroastrianism for the right reason. They suspect that seeking refuge in another religion, adopting the basic ideas of the Zoroastrian tradition and putting them into practice does not really do justice to the Zoroastrian religion.

Jenny Rose has drawn attention to the fact that priests or their assistants who do not originate from priestly families have recently begun to be trained in the USA. A training programme has started with at least one Parsi woman initiated as a *mobedyar*, as also one Iranian Zartoshti woman. The programme of study is similar to that of priestly candidates and it includes the study of languages and history, the reciting of prayers and becoming familiar with the rituals. Successful candidates will be initiated by non-practising Iranian *mobeds*. According to Rose, community gatherings of Zoroastrians in diaspora serve to bring individuals and families together and to encourage the continued recitation of the Avestan prayers[61].

Another development to be addressed is that many so-called para-Zoroastrians, or better 'neo-Zoroastrians', originating from the 'land of the Aryans' (meaning noble people) have become aware of their ancestral traditions[62]. Because they have lost direct contact with Zoroastrian thinking and are generally unaware of the deep historical roots of Zoroastrianism, they perform the Avestan rituals superficially. They unreservedly accept the authority of the *Gathas,* but not that of the Avestan liturgy. On the one hand, it is important to denounce the imposition of Islam in many Muslim countries. And to stress that these neo-Zoroastrians have chosen to become

---

60   Until recently, non-Zoroastrian women who marry Zoroastrian men become Zoroastrian, but this is not the case when Zoroastrian women marry non-Zoroastrian men.
61   Jenny Rose (2011, 230-231). Rose draws attention to a Zoroastrian website whose authors call upon Zoroastrian laity to become *saoshyants* through living their lives "in dedication to the vision of the world governed by righteousness, truth and benevolent thinking" (p. 230-31).
62   See *The Zoroastrian Diaspora: Religion and Migration*, ed. John Hinnells (Oxford, University Press, 2005) and *The Zoroastrian Flame: Exploring Religion, History and Tradition*, eds. Allan Williams, Sarah Stewart, Almut Hintze (London/ New York, Tauris, 2006).

Zoroastrians, maybe because they were left with no other choice. On the other hand, this wave of neo-Zoroastrianism can be welcomed as the outcome of a real choice, not one that is dictated by birth right or bloodlines.

Except if one considers that the restoration of pre-Islamic culture is a realistic proposition, the situation of neo-Zoroastrians will never be the same as that of 'original' Zoroastrians; which is why training programmes such those described above could well be the way forward. Maybe after all it is up to Zoroastrian laity and neo-Zoroastrians to show that not the provenance of individuals determines the way of life, nor the well-intended appropriation of religious prescriptions, but rather the contextualised continuation of the tradition. Witness the worldwide diaspora of Iranian and Parsi Zoroastrians, along with that of ethnic Aryans who were once Muslims, of the self-defined Zoroastrians who promote the idea of laity representatives continuing the tradition, and of the non-Zoroastrians who feel attracted to the religion or the way of life. Rather than a clear reference to an identity, neo-Zoroastrianism, or even mazdaphilia, could be used during the transition period as a more neutral term to designate what is obviously a growing interest in the philosophical and existential dimension of Zoroastrian thinking. Presented as an arch-practice it could possibly supersede the blood-and-soil ideology.

The revival of the Silk Road

Today, the word Iran triggers a number of divergent positions, mainly related to the geopolitical situation and the perceived opposition between East and West, which is constantly being reframed by different countries. The Eastern part of Iran, present-day Afghanistan, was part of the 'land of the Aryans', that in the 5th century BC stretched from India to Egypt. Many of the values that these people held in high regard were picked up by other cultures and religions, which is why it is less important to know the provenance of values like honesty, trust or integrity, than to reaffirm the need to uphold them through the ages. Paradoxically, in times of global tensions, more nations begin to lay claim to the Persian heritage, which will entail disagreements about historical facts.

The recent interest in the Silk Road, which the merchant caravans used to travel from the Far East to Istanbul and from Russia and China to Japan, is a case in point. From the 4th to the late 10th century, this network of land routes allowed merchants to cross borders and ply their trade in different countries with peoples from different cultures and religions. As a result of recent archaeological discoveries, Chinese scholars have begun to claim that Zoroastrian culture might not find its origin in the plateau region of Iran. They base their arguments on the existence of a culture that has to a large extent been forgotten, on the fact that Sogdians thrived from the 6th century BC to the 10th century AD. There is evidence of their existence during the period of the Silk Road, and research is ongoing.

Cyrus the Great conquered Sogdiana (now located in Tajikistan and Uzbekistan) in 540 BC. Archaeological research has confirmed the existence of a rich Sogdian culture and identified references to several Zoroastrian rituals. According to an inscription in Behistoun of Darius I, Sogdiana was the 18th province of the Achaemenids, a province also mentioned in the Vendidad as one of the territories under the aegis of Ahura Mazda. Funeral monuments of rich Sogdian merchants of the 6th and 7th century (e.g. funeral beds and sarcophagus found near Xian) or Zoroastrian fire temples like for example those referred to in Dunhuang confirm the existence of Sogdian Zoroastrians. A number of Zoroastrian temples were built in the early Tang period, "indicating there were Zoroastrian *magi* in China at that time"[63].

An extensive number of artifacts indicates the practice of a variant form of Zoroastrianism from the 5th to the 7th century AD, confirms the archaeologist Kersi Shroff. According to Shroff, "Sogdian religious practice can be considered to be a polytheist variant of Mazdeism, different from the later reformed Zoroastrianism of the Persian Sasanians"[64]. Shroff concentrated his research on the ancient regions of Sogdiana and Bactria. He refers to the many scholarly publications on the subject and to the importance of Samarkand, the capital of Sogdiana, where the king did not believe in the law of Buddha and where the people made sacrifices to fire.

Yipaer Aierken maintains that the Sogdians did not just disappear, but split into three main groups[65]. An interesting comparison is made between what Samarkand represented under the Tang dynasty of the 7th century and

---

63 Jenny Rose (2011, 152). See the chapter on Sogdian Zoroastrians of Central Asia.
64 Kersi Shroff, 'Ancient Sogdiana, "A Zoroastrian Stronghold"'. See: http://www.avesta.org/shroff/AncientSogdiana.pdf (2016).
65 A research paper by Dr. Yipaer Aierken (2017): https://www.researchgate.net/publication/322603609_Redefining_the_Art_and_Culture_of_Sogdians_From_Ethnic_Identity_Construction_to_Zoroastrianism_Who_Were_the_Sogdians

what Athens and Rome were to Western civilization. As to the importance of the Sogdians, Aierken reports that they were regarded as the most respected non-Chinese residents in China. And Jenny Rose observes that they were among the chief translators of Buddhist sutras into Chinese[66].

According to Boris Marshak, "the Sogdians inherited ancient Iranian traditions; Sogdian is an eastern Iranian language and the teachings of Zoroaster penetrated into Sogdiana at a very early stage"[67]. Nevertheless, "the majority of the Sogdians considered themselves Zoroastrians, but in their everyday life they mostly tried to receive protection from the more immediate gods of their family or their community and rarely appealed to Ahura Mazda". What is remarkable, says Marshak, is the contrast between the Zoroastrian funeral ritual and the non-Iranian appearance of Sogdian representations. He notices a difference in the funeral ritual, with in Zoroastrianism the corpse being exposed to vultures, while in Sogdiana the flesh is eaten by the dogs, after which the clean bones are collected and put into ceramic ossuaries.

---

66 Jenny Rose (2011, 148).
67 Boris I. Marshak, "The Sogdians and their homeland" in Annette L. Juliano and Judith A. Lerner, eds. *Monks and Merchants: Silk Road Treasures from Northwest China; Gansu and Ningxia, 4th to 7th Century,* New York, Harry N. Abrams and The Asia Society, 2001 (232). And p 233 for the following quotes.

PART FIVE
WHEN?

Call for justice

From reading the *Gathas* today, it appears that Zarathustra's call for justice is of all times. Seen as an archetypical expression of human life, his call has been renewed over and over again, pointing to the necessity of deepened awareness. The prevailing tone is that of a call for individual responsibility; one that is not addressed to a closed community or an ethnicity, but to virtually all the inhabitants of our planet. Zarathustra called for more wisdom in the future, a wisdom "enlightening or awaking all the living" (31,3). I refer to Dina McIntyre's chapter "A Teaching for all Mankind" and to a verse on blessings granted "unto all mankind" (51,20)[1]. Other than a proclamation of truth, of words spoken by one man and forever valuable, this testimony is a call for good understanding of the basic values of life around the world, appealing to each individual.

As has become clear in the previous chapters, Zarathustra's first concern was not to disseminate a new religion, but to offer a reply to malicious deception. He called upon each person's sense of responsibility, because he was saddened by the injustices of which humans are capable. He testified

---

[1] As Dina McIntyre underlines, Zarathustra is addressed "all those of the same temperament", who experience Wisdom "as a friend". This is potentially true for all beings seen from the perspective that Wisdom is a gift: "Wisdom's support is not limited to a particular group". It is "a gift – it does not have to be earned (…) and a bountiful generosity that is part of the true order of existence". McIntyre raises then this question: "How does Wisdom support?". By referring to verse 49,1, she concludes that "Wisdom does not support us by placing us in a harm-free bubble" nor by "abolishing difficult experiences", since these "are the way we grow". This means that instead of nurturing anger, guilt or depression, we can respond to what we experience as harmful, unjust or destructive by ourselves, supporting ourselves the true order of existence.

to what falsehood can lead to, to the fact that it prevents humans from flourishing, from achieving their full growth. It is not a call for the brutal and definitive eradication of all injustices, but an invitation to resist them each time again. It cannot be said often enough that resistance implies recognising our own wrongdoings, and not only those of others, so that we are able to confront them in a timely and appropriate manner. This proto-ethical and proto-ecological call is directed towards all the individuals who are intent on protecting what is precious. Zarathustra insisted on this point: "Oh, women and men who will unite, understand properly the words I am saying to you and remember them. Integrate the proper understanding in your life" (53,5).

At the end of the eighteenth century in revolutionary Europe, the call for more justice produced the motto 'liberty, equality, fraternity'. So, it is hardly surprising that the discovery of Zarathustra's thoughts played an important role in that specific process of enlightenment. On the one hand, the news that his teachings had been salvaged and were in the process of being translated put paid to the legends and rumours. On the other hand, the news also gave rise to a political power struggle. France and England opposed one another on the authenticity of the documents and furthermore, the scientific pioneer and translator Anquetil-Duperron was not given due merit for his efforts. Strangely enough, the Zoroastrian appeal for more justice was exposed to its antithesis and the call for more justice, implying the denunciation of malpractices, prompted those who felt attacked to counterattack in response.

The young Anquetil-Duperron, who had lived in India from 1755 to 1761, arrived at the conclusion that Zarathustra's way of life was consistently observed in the daily lives of the members of the Parsi communities. He was horrified by the cruelty of the first conquerors, by their mercantile mentality and by the reasons they gave to bring freedom, even though these fanatic conquerors were only motivated by personal interest. He became involved in the dispute over "the Orientals being another species of man than the Europeans", and rejected the allegation that they were barbarians who had to be freed from despotism and local tyrannical governments[2].

---

2   Abraham Hyacinthe Anquetil-Duperron, *Législation orientale*, Amsterdam, Marc-Michel Rey (1778, 87). His indictment of Western knowledge, politeness, civilised conduct was not just motivated by contempt for his own culture; it was an attempt to encourage arm-chair scientists to open their eyes to the richness of

In his defence of the Orient and in praising the people whom he found to be honest and respectful, he denounced the concept of oriental despotism invented by Montesquieu and the messianic voluntarism of philosophers like Diderot and Voltaire. Because of his close relations with the indigenous people, he began to stand up against European superiority and hypocrisy[3]. His anti-colonialism and first denunciation of 'crimes against humanity' are here referred to not to chastise European domination, but to recall Alexander Dow's forebodings of destruction and premonition that "this civilisation will vanish from our hands". Not so much the equality between all peoples was emphasised by Anquetil-Duperron as the unity of humanity.

Renewing the message

In this book, I do not wish to pile up the accusations against the many instances of Western barbarism that resulted in peoples being robbed and dehumanized throughout the centuries of colonization. Neither do I wish to simply provide an overview of the use and misuse of the name of Zarathustra, such as occurred in France, England or Germany, and of his recuperation at the end of the eighteenth century. The focus here is on how and whether this arch-knowledge and primal insights can be revived each time again, especially in the context of ecological urgencies and endangered freedoms with which present-day society is faced. What is needed is not the authority of famous thinkers and celebrities, but personal motivation to individually put our ideas into practice and renew our attempts to become more consistent in our interaction with others.

History shows that bringers of peace will be confronted with violence and must themselves be good practitioners of self-examination, of the tripartite motto and its implied resistance. Zarathustra himself was well aware of this, and when he felt let down, he cried out his despair. But he also found a response in the deafening silence and requested the blessing of perseverance and the support of strength divine. By chanting praises (50,4) he hoped that the blessings would "come in shape of help".

---

        other peoples who are anything but barbarian. If the ancient Greeks were to return, he stated, they would treat us as barbarians (p. 178).

3   Lucette Valensi describes Anquetils' voluntary poverty, the bad treatment he suffered in France after his return, and the denial of his monumental work as a precursor. https://www.persee.fr/doc/rhr_0035-1423_1995_num_212_4_1250

Discouraged by the absence of help from his friends, he asked: "When shall the days of trueness dawn?" (46,3). "When will dedication come (...) and rewarding service, bringing peace and rest?" (48,11).

The repeated 'when' is a signal of Zarathustra's yearning. It is a request awaiting a reply, as he opened up to a "gesture answering my song[4], this help that bears me upwards to thy light (50,5). Reaffirmed hereby is the confidence and hope implicit in the *Gathas*; this openness to a possible connection between heaven and earth. And along with it, the need for protection of abused humans and of nature, which was already a fact more than 3000 years ago. With reference to the history of the planet, the recent and short appearance of humans on earth has not shown to be an adequate response to the initial potential of life. If Zarathustra is right, the long process of emancipation ahead includes our reply to the damage caused by false leaders, addressed to whomsoever takes advantage of the weak, including nature itself.

The threat posed by human beings who are now able to destroy all life on earth culminated with the explosion of the first atomic bomb. This may have been an eye-opener for scientists and politicians, but has so far failed to have a real impact on what constitutes the core issue of human existence: can we continue to fool ourselves that we humans are in a position to control the universe? What we need to challenge is the idea we have of our freedom. A new and revised version must be developed, enriched by the basic knowledge experienced in this proto-philosophy: a dishonest life does not make us happy, not because we have failed to tell the truth, but because we refuse to dismiss a deceptive image of freedom and so continue to be wrong about what will make us happy and free. Bad faith is self-deception (Sartre), and a voluntary flight before the social impact of untrueness. Zarathustra warned that "a lie is a destroyer of life" (53,6), not so as to provide an ethical guideline or a precept we can blindly follow, but to make us realise that "the pleasure obtained by deceiving others is a source of pain and suffering" (53,6).

---

4   Let us be reminded that Nietzsche also wrote songs. In the last aphorism of *Joyful Science,* he declares that his knowledge is not that of a scholar, but of a singer, and he chooses to finish his work with 'The Songs of Prince Free-as-a-Bird (*Lieder des Prinzen Vogelfrei*), songs that were put to music by the Belgian composer Janpieter Biesemans (2015).

Part Five: When?

Ignored freedom

As we have seen, free choice does not primarily concern the choice between moral good and evil, but the act of choosing itself. To respect the primordial choice means that we choose to say yes to choosing, to the tripartite motto, to the choice of giving precedence to the tendency towards trueness and to fight untrueness. This quest is not that of a specific culture or era; it is the quest of all those who agree to account for their actions. Thus spoke Zarathustra: "Consult your wisdom and choose". If you are in doubt, expose yourself to the "flamboyant fire of wisdom" (51,9) and "communicate with your inner self and gain intuition" (53,3). Wisdom can unite people, assigning "each one's duty unto each", which is a way of becoming more self-reliant (53,4).

What we need in the so-called post-truth era is a social practice that allows individuals to acknowledge their inaccuracies on the path towards a more fulfilling life. In order to turn a disrupted society into what is beneficial for everyone, we need to become more humane thanks to the flexibility of the discerning mind in its daily struggle with the friend and the foe within. Every time the mask of integrity is dropped, this does not cause a sense of failure, since it is seen as an incentive to take up the timeless challenge of what it means to be a human being. What we need is increased awareness of the existence of the two opposite tendencies inside each one of us, which allows us to give preference to truer modes of being by respecting the tripartite motto.

We have communication highways, social media, technologies that enable us to exchange ideas on freedom as a kind of responsibility and to inspire our friends, but we also need to put our good intentions into practice. Along with the message and the medium, a spirit of reinvigoration can be passed on, preferably indirectly and creatively, either by a minority of thinkers, or by means of direct and public action addressed to all. The question of numbers, of how many are involved in the process, plays an important role in the following chapters. All the same, it is not my intention to present Zarathustra as the prophet of the world or as an exemplary figure, but to borrow his thoughts in order to fight mental rigidity and paralysis.

In the history of philosophy, this ignored freedom which Zarathustra pointed at was picked up by famous thinkers who welcomed the new vision on responsibility. As we have seen, the Greek philosophers were aware of the antagonistic principle ruling the world and knew about the acknowledgment of the internal fight between the two tendencies. But, with the birth of metaphysics, this was pushed into the background. The Parmenidean principle of the difference between being and appearances, between perception and thought, received all the attention. Also, with the Sophists, among whom eloquence triumphed, the focus shifted towards opinions, rather than on what actually takes place. All too often, the act of speaking was justified and the rhetorical abuse of words was a fact.

The inappropriate use of our intelligence was regularly rebuked and a new era was announced in modern times, when poets like Goethe admitted "two souls, alas, dwell in my breast". Goethe was a forerunner of Nietzsche's philosophy on the limits of human existence. To dare admit that you are a theatre of contradictions was seen as a way of not hiding behind moral codes, as an honest answer to the dissatisfaction with life[5]. What counted was to give meaning to life on earth by promoting life-affirming values and this-worldliness, rather than the abnegation of the body and the promise of fulfilment in another world. This line of thinking, including the liberation from falsehood and deception, made Goethe welcome some Eastern viewpoints on life.

Goethe was influenced by the figure of Zarathustra and expressed one of the first criticisms of Western ideology. He believed it was high time to advocate a humane global philosophy. In his *West-Eastern Divan*, he interposed Persian terms in the verses to do justice to Hafiz, the Oriental poet he was inspired by. Besides, Emerson and Baudelaire also detected in Hafiz the same Zoroastrian call for liberation. He influenced Nietzsche, according to whom Hafiz was a true free thinker. Let us remember that freethinking in this mindset referred to the aforementioned ignored freedom and not to truth which should be formed on the basis of logic, reason and empiricism, as a reaction to tradition, dogma or revelation. In the post-truth era, freedom may possibly announce the pre-trueness era in the form of responsible responses.

---

5   The analysis of one-ness turning into two-ness is based in my study on Zarathustra in French on one of the verses sung by Nietzsche's Prince Free-as-a-Bird: "Then, suddenly, woman friend! (*freundin*) one turned into two – And Zarathustra walked past me".

Part Five: When?

Nietzsche's Zarathustra

According to the historians of Zoroastrian religion, Nietzsche's Zarathustra and Zarathushtra Spitama seem to have little in common. As a philologist and scholar of oriental religions, Nietzsche was familiar with Persian thinking[6]. Unlike Thomas Hyde or Voltaire and the efforts to turn the Persian prophet into a founder of a world religion, he picked up on the aspect of unconscious lying. Nietzsche warned against professional philosophers who neglect the existential dimension of philosophy, the lived experiences that exceed logical thinking. His suspicion of philosophers who only appear to be transparent, was a reminder of the ruin awaiting them if they turn their backs on more truthfulness. In *On Truth and Lies in a Non-moral Sense* (1873), he states: "For so far we have heard only of the duty which society imposes in order to exist: to be truthful means to employ the usual metaphors. Thus, to express it morally, this is the duty to lie according to a fixed convention, to lie with the herd and in a manner binding upon everyone".

We know for a fact that Nietzsche started his studies on oriental religions (Brahmanism, Rig-Veda, Buddhism, Islam) and on Persian culture in 1875. Undoubtedly, he should be given credit for reviving the flame of Persian thinking, for having invented a new language to do so. Above all, he was intrigued by Zarathustra, but felt the need to accuse him of having created "this most fateful of all errors, morality", of having invented good and evil[7]. In order to set things right and present himself as the first immoralist, he gave life to a figure that bore the Persian homonym. Apart from the fact that this presentation did not correspond with what the *Gathas* convey, Nietzsche succeeded in exploring the idea of going beyond good and evil. In *Thus spoke Zarathustra*, he grasped the revolutionary movement of the Persian Zarathustra, to think for oneself, rather than to hold on to authoritarian prescriptions.

---

6   Claudio Mutti explains that Nietzsche, apart from his interest in Oriental philosophy (Rig-Veda, Buddha) and Greek Antiquity (he read Plutarch and studied the doctrine of Zarathustra), learned about Zoroastrianism through the translations of Martin Haug, but also through some of the essays of Ralph Waldo Emerson and the book by the orientalist Friedrich Spiegel *Eranische Alterthumskunde*. Mutti is the author of *L'unità dell'Eurasia* (Genova, Effepi, 2008), see further note 12.

7   *Ecce homo*, 'Why I am a Destiny" 3.

What is characteristic of both Zarathustras is the need to call on man's responsibility, to activate human wisdom from within, and not to leave things in the hands of leaders who make bad use of their power. Nietzsche reacted to the herd instinct of decadent European leaders and to the hypocritical representatives of the church. He displaced the accent from discursive truth to actual, existential power. Rather than to rely on persuasive speaking, on rhetorical convictions, his philosophy expresses the experience of life in a movement toward trueness. The self-improvement of humans which Nietzsche had in mind was intended as a liberation process from moralizing Western tradition and an empowerment of individuals who exercise in truthfulness.

The 'death of God' was indeed not intended to be a triumphant murder by humans who felt superior and tried to erase transcendental reality, but as a wake-up call to creatively take one's life into one's own hands. Benjamin Fondane picked up on this interpretation of the dead God and defended the idea that Nietzsche's instigation only concerned a moral God. This Romanian poet-thinker, who died in a concentration camp in 1944, dedicated a chapter in his *Unhappy Consciousness* to Nietzsche's 'supreme cruelty'[8]. Fondane was not scandalised by the death of God and agreed on the destructive dimension of morals with its paralysing effects. The moralising dimension of philosophy, according to him, missed the encouragement not to flee from reality. He accused modern philosophers of over-reliance on the rational mind and putting too little trust in the creative act of dealing with reality. They appease their conscience, said Fondane, and try to convince, rather than daring to descend into the abysses of existence. He incited his readers to listen to the objections of the other 'me', of otherness, and not to resign themselves to false peace.

Fondane was inspired by the mobilising Nietzschean spirit[9]. The 'will for power', a primary concept of Nietzsche's thinking, inspired him not to find comfort in the perdition of a passive lifestyle, but to go beyond the small self to build a consistent one. From this viewpoint, Nietzsche did not develop an ethics of the strong, rather of strongwilled, decisive, perseverant

---

8   Benjamin Fondane, *La Conscience malheureuse* (Paris, Verdier/Non Lieu, 2013).
9   Fondane invited his readers to be brave enough to 'dare' not to distort reality and to stop presenting the creative act as a remedy against excessive rational, conceptual and instrumental thinking. He incited them, instead of fleeing, to dare to live in the real world, to be, to re-energise oneself with real and genuine experiences.

persons. Neither did he promote an egocentric superhuman (*Übermensch*), who develops a will for power and overcomes his weaknesses; the idea of superseding frailty was more about beating complacency than about self-sacrifice. This is why, as Nietzsche observed, only exceptional persons will put their lives at risk and engage in what appears to be impossible.

According to Nietzsche, throughout the history of humanity, only exceptional figures have ever succeeded in playing a role that could make humanity progress. Nietzsche's Zarathustra probably fulfilled that part of the play – a role he could not ascribe to everyone. Only he who overcomes decadency and holds onto a truer mode of being is 'noble', like the Aryan people. No biological connotation is attached to the word aryan; 'superhuman' individuals do not descend from a race[10]. The future man, thus Nietzsche, is capable of 'saying yes' (*Jasagen*) to life. To 'say yes' primarily means that one stops distorting reality. This 'saying yes' that he highlighted was enthusiastically welcomed by a whole generation of youngsters who discovered his texts at the end of the second World War. Nevertheless, contrary to what can be found in the *Gathas*, Nietzsche called on a minority of individuals who deploy themselves optimally and not on all individuals.

Eurasia

To come true in honesty, Nietzsche said, is part of the individual existential process – a process that led towards a new era. If the one truth does not exist, if it cannot be tied down, then it is dynamic like the sun that rises and sets, that conceals and unveils. A dynamic vision of life also includes the balance between two competing creative energies, called the Apollonian and the Dionysian. To live life as an artist demands that we be ready to reside from time to time in the existential cavern, with its different degrees of darkness. This is essential, provided the cavern has openings through which the light can enter. Nietzsche's saying 'yes' to life implies that we cannot untie the knots of the past, but that we are willing to readjust

---

10   See Koenraad Elst, 'The Indo-European, Vedic and post-Vedic meanings of "Arya" ', *Vedic Venues 2*, Kolkata (2013), 57-77. Most noteworthy is the following statement: "If the word *Arya* had not become tainted by the colonial and racist use of its Europeanised form *Aryan*, the chances are that by now it would have replaced the word *Hindu* (which many Hindus resent as a Persian exonym unknown to Hindu scripture) as the standard term of Hindu self-reference".

them in another way. It is the significant element on which both figures of Zarathustra accord.

Nietzsche shook up his audience by telling them that the history of Western philosophy was permeated by idealistic and spiritualist goals. Much attention went to thinking and reasoning, which not only produced a plurality of opinions, but allowed the tyrants of opinions to distract the attention from what was actually taking place. They stimulated meek obedience and docility, instead of addressing the real issues of daily life, like poverty, illness, old age. Nietzsche believed the decadence of the West could receive an answer in considering Europe and Asia as being complementary. Albeit an interesting political idea, the birth of a new humanity, of a new world, referred to a successful synthesis, which would only be possible, as he stated, if the Dionysian world of India could be accepted by Apollonian Greek thought[11]. Less well known is the name *Eurasia*, which Nietzsche used to advance the freedom to engage in a dream directed to the East, more so than to the West[12].

In *Ecce homo*, he had explained that Europe could no longer limit itself to "small nationalist states" and he had denounced the decadence of the "national neurosis of which Europe suffers". In response to this "small politics", he proposed the unification of Europe on the basis of inevitable cultural and economic exchanges and of a mixed European race[13]. And he considered Europeans to be "the utmost indebted inheritors of thousands of years of old European mind". Indo-European cultures, Nietzsche argued, were the cradle of Western thinking and the latter should not become their graveyard. Therefore, the renewal of 'Western' thinking is meaningful only if the 'old world' is rightfully honoured.

Nietzsche did not turn the East into a remedy for decadent Western civilization, but he tried to reestablish the distorted world view, not by inventing a superior Western being, but by rehabilitating what had been twisted, and by proposing another kind of humanity. It is here that a passage

---

11   *The Birth of Tragedy* (section 20).
12   On Eurasia, see Claudio Mutti, "L'unità dell'Eurasia nella prospettiva di Friedrich Nietzsche" (2009). https://www.eurasia-rivista.com/lunita-delleurasia-nella-prospettiva-di-friedrich-nietzsche
13   *Joyful Science*, aphorism 377. We are, says Nietzsche, "good Europeans, the heirs of Europe, but we also have an obligation as over-wealthy heirs of a spiritual millennium of Europe".

in *Ecco homo* takes on a prophetic appearance: "The day that truth will engage in a struggle against the thousand years old lie, we will experience disruptions, seismic convulsions, tectonic shocks we have never imagined and which will displace mountains and valleys. The idea of politics will then have resorbed in the war of individuals. All forms of power of the ancient society will have vanished, since they are based on the lie". This quotation on the decline of Western decadence is to be read as the logical necessity for a new world to emerge.

On the one hand, Nietzsche's dream was apocalyptic and based on the idea that the 'last man' will be replaced by the 'superhuman'. The 'last men' are nihilist, tired of life, and have become indifferent, passive and ignorant of the possibilities to overcome smallness, laziness and apathy. So, the superhuman is an answer to mediocrity. On the other hand, the figure of Zarathustra which Nietzsche admired was someone he himself could never become. Was he ultimately deluded by the prognosis that Western nihilistic spirit had become too decadent to cultivate human life? Was he disappointed that humans failed in their purpose to put creativity first? Nevertheless, he remained true to the difference between claiming to possess the truth and being true, and never hid his weaknesses and contradictory ideas. He spent his last years in illness and solitude and proclaimed that the philosopher is not someone who possesses the truth, but someone who remains faithful to trueness. He could only hold on to what and whom he had become, instead of pretending to be someone else.

Remain true to the earth

One hundred years after Nietzsche's philosophy, we see that not the 'death of God' is the event "too great, too distant, too remote from the multitude's capacity for comprehension", but the 'death of Man', his lack of responsibility, which moreover is the cause of the death of some many other life forms. Nietzsche raised the issue of "the multitude's capacity for comprehension" and did not trust what we today call the masses, in their capacity to rightly understand the will to power. His belief in the superhuman being was based on the idea that only a minority will succeed in superseding the small self. Unless Europeans renew their thinking (which is too rational, too moralizing, too metaphysical) and deal with reality rather than being entranced by possessing the truth, decadent Europeanism cannot be saved, Nietzsche claimed. The qualities he ascribed to future superhuman beings depended on a new configuration of life based on the creativity of the few who "remain true to the earth"[14].

This idea of "remaining true to the earth" reflects an alternative way of life, in which contempt for the body is replaced by Dionysian aspects. Nietzsche, in his depiction of unfathomed superhuman capacities, urged his readers to "remain true to the earth and not to believe those who speak of supernatural hope". The centre of Nietzsche's interest was to reduce the impact of Apollonian, rational thinking and to overcome the neglect of the body, because of metaphysical speculations or religious normativity. But we find some weak points in his quest. The idea of combining the Dionysian world of India with Apollonian Greek thought was based on the body-mind dualism[15] and on the concept of eternal recurrence, two elements resembling traditional metaphysics. Moreover, typical of modern and post-modern philosophy is its endless criticism of Western thinking, its formulation of alternative thoughts in the best of cases, with the emphasis being put on generating new ideas, but with the major weakness of forgetting human's subordination to nature.

As a matter of fact, Nietzsche's perspective is again inscribed in an anthropocentric frame of thought. His anthropocentrism has its roots in an Indo-European way of life, with a horizon of human beings with superhuman qualities. His great merit is undoubtedly his courage to truthfully reflect inner tensions, contradictions and personal inconsistencies. Rather than to engage in political discussions and to verbally polemicise against wrongdoers, he showed how deep mankind has fallen and how art and creativity can generate a new humanity. Still, Nietzsche seems to forget that the overflowing generosity of creativity is not self-evident, which is why we cannot hold him to account for not giving due consideration to ecological matters that were not yet a predominant issue. But this doesn't alter the fact that he did not consider nature's capacity to recover from brutal human interventions.

If the Western nihilistic spirit was based on the lie, as Nietzsche advanced and if he was deluded by the smallness of the 'last' human beings, then his anthropocentric vision of the future is superseded today by the fact that there is a destructive side to the unrestrained creativity impulse of

---

14 *Thus spoke Zarathustra*, Introduction, 3.
15 Nietzsche admired the texts of Mani; *The Antichrist*, aphorism 56 and 57.

superhuman individuals who take the idea of eternal recurrence for granted or who rely on nature's capacity to regenerate. For this reason, the concept of the superhuman appears today also to be based on the lie. Nietzsche, in his preoccupation for humanity, failed to take into account that humans should not abuse of what is put at their disposal and should consider due care for our planet. If his Zarathustra figure spoke with animals, it was because he could not get a response from humans. Most probably he cherished the beauty of nature when he journeyed to Italy and France, but life's generosity seemed self-evident and was not based on cautious interaction with the environment[16].

Nietzsche led a rather ascetic life as he distanced himself from the academic establishment and bourgeois society, but his asceticism was not a choice based on respect for fragile nature. His main reason for calling for a consistent way of life had everything to do with fighting questionable morals and metaphysics, and very little with choosing to respect nature's generosity. Although the first signs of industrialism were noticeable and Nietzsche himself wrote this line: "In truth, man is a polluted river. One must be a sea to receive a polluted river without becoming defiled", this does not mean he was concerned about a sustainable environment[17]. Today, to take nature for granted is to have little regard for what is life-giving; it even includes failing to show due respect to the life-giving capacity of women[18]. Respect for nature cannot arise from the virtue of abundance, since the conditions that make abundance sustainable are to be taken into consideration.

Seen from this angle, by bearing in mind that all resources are scarce and subject to conditions, Zarathustra Spitama was more consistently in line with nature's fragility and human vulnerability. If the necessity of the creativity impulse is to be endorsed in the ages to come, we cannot ignore

---

16 Nietzsches relation to nature would be an interesting subject of study. I refer to aphorism 280 in *Joyful Science*: "We would like to transform ourselves into stones and plants". And to *Also sprach Zarathustra* (Part IV, 'The Song of Melancholy'): "I love you, my dear animals". Of course, the issue of sexual difference could not be left out, nor his many controversial observations on women, whom he considered gave birth to superhumans.
17 *Thus spoke Zarathustra*, Introduction, 3.
18 True, philosophers tend to shut themselves off from society, but if possible they rely on women for practical matters:). Much has been written on Nietzsche's misogyny. I prefer not to emphasise the issue of gender, but Nietzsche's love of distance. Even if it is a feeble reaction to Christian 'love of nearness', the concept of 'star' friendship is supposed to include a certain magic in the exercise of keeping the object of desire at a distance.

the chain reactions and counter-reactions with regard to environmental sustainability. Less certain today than hundred years ago is the carrying capacity of the earth and the earth's food-producing capacity. For the planet to survive human intervention, we do not only require ecological design, sustainability and innovation, but we need a mentality shift, a readiness to give all due consideration to the planet and to the rich variety of species that was once the object of human enthusiasm. The very fact that species threatened with extinction are not helped by the invention of new concepts designed by man to improve his condition could trigger a response. Are we left with lonesome individuals who dare to express diverging opinions, but lack care and caution in their relations?

Relapse into non-life?

Transposed to our era and translated into the language of the *Gathas*, we arrive at this finding. Both Zarathustras denounce the condition of non-life and accuse spiritual non-leadership as a serious misdeed in the evolution of mankind: a misdeed of the power-hungry who mask what is real and disguise what is unreal. Sadly, in his fight against decadence, Nietzsche became the victim of what he had warned against. No one can tell whether his mental breakdown was the result of an enduring chaotic situation, of his tormented consciousness or whether he victimised himself because he was an outcast. Was he excluded from society or did he exclude himself from it? Was he able to strike the right balance between the Dionysian and Apollonian impulses in his effort to give more impetus to the body (the Dionysian) than to the mind (the Apollonian)? Did he fail to detach himself from the body-mind dualism to which all Western philosophers adhered until the 20th century?

Failure, illness, misery belong to a truthful existence, but one cannot put one's trust in them as a guideline. If contradictions and inaccuracies are part of life's process, they are instruments to proceed and are not meant to have the final say. Spitama's warnings against the relapses into non-life hold little irony, scepticism or rhetoric, because they are founded not so much on verbal statements, but on the primordial choice that one is willing to choose over and over again. We are told we should not victimise ourselves because we made wrong choices, but we can break the stalemate and trust ourselves to make right choices in the future. A durable yes implies that we are ready to say yes to the tripartite motto, instead of relapsing in bitterness.

Which is why these warnings can be read today as a recommendation not to fall back into what causes resentment, depression or distrust; as advice to be watchful with regard to the so-called comfort zone, which is a constant menace in our take-away society.

Our consumer societies offer a form of well-being in which people are deluded into thinking that there are rapid solutions to all problems and that seeking comfort and security is the main purpose in life. This description of non-life today includes the danger to which we are exposed coming from organisations that gain control over the media, from exploitative governments and multinationals with a power far greater than that of national governments. In order to hide their greed, the 'men at the top' infiltrate the social media and create the impression that migration is the true cause of the current impoverishment of Western societies. Indeed, democracy-based societies are threatened by the power-hungry who conceal their best self-interest and whose representatives twist and pervert the rules of the financial and economic world, appropriate natural resources and renewable energies and disrupt the social safety net for which our forefathers gave their lives. Is it really life-giving to aim for a luxurious life without personal implication, to be surrounded by beautiful objects without being personally creative, to stay in a confined and secured home with hardly any friendly contacts, to be locked-in or in hiding?

The real threat implied in this relapse into non-life is not the downfall of so-called Western values, but the looming danger of ethnic, racial, religious and social segregation. The values for which so many successive generations have fought were supposed to make us understand that a multicultural substrate is – biologically and mentally – specific to people from all over the world. As DNA analysis or anthropological research on values and morals will invariably show, we are all made up of elements from different nations and continents. So, when suspicion and distrust of others gains increase and protectionism takes over, people generally listen to those who advice not to take any risk. This is exactly how life then easily relapses into non-life, which inspires people to be constantly on their guard. They fear that the onetime colonised civilizations are eager to seize the flag and disrupt Western democracies from the outside or from within. The propaganda-based fear that it is pay-back time triggers a countermovement fed by neo-nationalists, who forcefully defend their 'own' native territories, while deprived landowners spread the news about how their properties were plundered.

All this is happening while the planet is being impacted as never before by fires and floods. Will these natural disasters increase our awareness of the mismanagement of our planet; will they positively influence the way North and South, East and West deal with the issue? With regard to the most urgent problems, to divide the planet into different parts and to use regression in the West as an argument to prove that advancement can only come from the East, or to exacerbate the fear that the North will be overrun by the South will not prove very helpful. False leaders will continue to conceal the huge profits that come from exploitation and warfare and to stigmatise migration as the major cause of global decline; they will continue to deny that it is precisely exploitation and warfare that drive people to migrate to better places. It seems reasonable to assume that if people were able to rely on an environment that could support them and to which they could contribute, they would probably not leave their homes and families behind.

Contemporary approach

For the first time in history, the planet has started to reject the human species. Humans become destructive intruders when, on a global scale, they begin to deny life on earth to other living beings. When human beings lose their earthly roots, they also seem to lose their sense of belonging to the world, their cosmic roots. As a result, they become less capable of putting an end to their own violent interventions; the phrase to tackle the problem at its roots is emptied of all meaning. What we are facing is declining readiness to actively take part in a regenerative process. With global issues becoming increasingly complex, the question arises whether a small number of individuals will suffice to address the common interest of saving the planet, even though we already know that severe ecological imbalances will occur in the near future.

Maybe Zarathustra's message has become obsolete in times such as these, when the earth has become an object, full of useful materials; an object to be saved from destruction, rather than a living being in need of being nurtured. In times such as these, when we are painfully aware of the non-life we are organising, it may be unrealistic to turn to ideas formulated ages ago. Can we seriously assume that proto-philosophical thoughts will only gain attention after a series of ecological disasters? Do we really believe that a period of daily scarcity and misery will make us more prepared to consider these words on mother earth, "who is our refuge; and who brings soul-strength and life-renewed" (48,6). Anyhow, the apathetic proposition formulated at the turn of the third millennium of the disappearance of humans on earth which will allow the planet to survive, is obviously the reverse of what Zarathustra had in mind. Human life on earth will not just simply vanish, however much defeatism there is. Such a scenario implies enormous suffering, not to mention the destructive impact on so many known and unknown lifeforms.

In order to understand that mother earth should be protected from those who claim to save it, without paying respect to its generosity, we need an existential climate change. Let us have a look at this proposition: to cultivate the earth is to improve justice. It is based on Zarathustra's claim that "the earth is fundamental", both for growth and mental strength (48,5). This idea is so basic that we are almost tempted to disregard it and to pay little attention to the fact that self-esteem grows in accordance with honest work. Today, millions of people simply know what is good for them on a basic level. How regenerating a good night's sleep can be and how great it is to ingest healthy food; how encouraging it is to collectively engage in less harmful lifestyles. Is it possible that these very same people choose to have a bad influence on one another? Have they forgotten what their forefathers knew intuitively? Is it so hard to see that people, blinded by the dullness of consumption, are being lulled into a false sense of what is meaningful and are failing to realise that putting on a new face to achieve a better life will simply not be enough?

Zarathustra did not dream of a perfect, ideal world, but convinced real people of how important it is to engage in the common project of bringing more justice to all that is. He really believed that "the holy plan is to make good decisions" (49,6) and to make others see that striving to understand is the way to reach true life (51,19). This was his reasoning: the world of plants and animals is already perfect, but human life is only potentially perfect. Human life being imperfect and unfinished gives humans a good reason to make full use of their regenerating potential in a proper way. Maybe they feel compelled to do so, but they are actually given the choice to do so. If they fail to use their potential, they become themselves obstacles to the other creatures on earth that try come to completion. "So, let them strive with thought and word and deed, Mazda, to satisfy – let each one choose deeds of goodness" (53,2), Zarathustra stated. The choice is about the difference between on the one hand, longing for the bliss of Mazda

(51,20), through chants to be led into light (51,16); and on the other, to "not foster our mother earth and behave worse than any of the bad" (51,6).

A contemporary approach of Zarathustra's wisdom leads to the translation into a present-day language of this ecological love of wisdom, so that we rightly understand the meaning of cultivating the earth as a strength-giving activity, maintaining a respectful and praising relationship with what is so generously put at our disposal. Zarathustra defended 'life before death', repeated that there is a regenerative element that humans can find in the self-regulation of trueness, by following the tripartite motto, and in their dedication, which engenders strength to start anew after each possible failure. Occasionally, joy is generated in perseverance, in fighting inaccurate attitudes; and gratitude follows new chances, new attempts, new hope. To reach 'endless light' refers to the countless opportunities in the returning desire to achieve more wisdom, which is tied to the condition of striving together: "Let each one strive" and bear in mind to "bring down good thinking in your lives" (53,5). The endless light that reaches us does not so much imply a reward, but is a perfect reflection of the atopic condition of light that shines in darkness. This is possibly one of the most profound messages of oriental thinking: not only the light of day, shining gloriously, is the creative and nurturing element, but also the night that gives birth to the day.

Philosophical ecology

It has been suggested that Zoroastrianism was the first Green movement[19]. Now that the world is waking up to the primacy of environmental protection, a renewed ecological love of wisdom, an ecosophy awaits humanity. The first requirement is that humans liberate themselves from the postulation that they are the masters of the world. Human beings act in an all but humanely manner when they think of themselves as the crowning glory of creation. Instead of adapting the planet to their wishes at the expense of future generations, they should understand that one single action has

---

19 On the internet, there are several articles by Zoroastrian scholars who seek to characterise Zoroastrianism as the world's first environmental religion. But there are also opponents to this view who refer to rituals that are in opposition to contemporary science. My intention here is not to engage in this discussion and to let each reader find out whether this proto-philosophy can provide answers to the present-day ecological urgency.

an incidence on its further dynamics. To adopt a position in the world as responsible beings requires respect for nature's self-regulation. To enter into the cosmic play of being true to oneself is a personal commitment. At the same time, it is a contribution to the unique project of life; and it is unique not because of some higher value or because of the sovereign position of humans, but because of the singularity of each circumspect way of handling things. This way, 'human' and 'humane' become qualifications of the way we treat others and everything that surrounds us.

For the planet to survive human intervention, next to technological and economic innovation, we need a philosophical ecology, indeed an ecosophy to map out our responsibility. Let us again consider this sentence from the *Gathas*: "A good environment in which one engages to serve the fecundity of the earth is the most beautiful price to gain for humanity" (34,14). The Zoroastrian practice of respect for the four elements is known to put the environment, on which life depends, in a central position. From the beginning of mankind, being aware of the interaction with the environment and with each other offered good prospects for warding off the inclination to disregard the nutrient cycle of life. Zarathustra, who was struck by just how wonderful the joys of the earth felt, could not believe that the people around him acted as if they were deprived of reflection. Was he wrong in assuming that his own feeling of admiration was shared by all? In fact, what they neglected was the dynamic force present in nature's regeneration process. But how could he make them pay attention to nature and discover its most interesting evolutionary drive?

For us to understand how this approach is relevant with regard to current ecological issues, a brief outline of the current situation may be helpful. On the one hand, climate change skeptics, deniers or catastrophists, concede that a number of countries will sooner or later be faced with huge challenges to adapt to largely unpredictable new situations brought about not only by global warming, but also by food shortages and migratory waves. The lack of scientific consensus in the global warming controversy has given rise to a denial industry, which organises disinformation campaigns intended to increase uncertainties about the global harmful impact. The weak element in the debate on climate change is once again the absence of human accountability in consumerist societies.

Climate change optimists, on the other hand, tell us we should wait for the results of renewable solar and wind energy, of the efforts of decarbonized electricity and transport, and trust scientific progress, technological innovation and economic entrepreneurship. As a matter of fact, in the so-called post-industrialisation era, we continue to think in terms of economic growth, exploitation and success, while the planet itself appears to be concerned with the welfare and prosperity of all that is, including non-human forms of life on earth, and especially non-organic life or at least what was designated as such until recently. Humans deny the risks associated with an instrumental view and turn a blind eye to the very fact that a resolute change of mentality involves no risk at all.

A worldwide wave of indignation, caused by the political denial of ecological disasters spontaneously gained strength in Europe. It lay dormant for a few decennia and then suddenly surfaced in March 2019. The movement Youth4Climate in Belgium was directed against climate change denial by politicians and was fed by the fear of many children and youngsters with an apocalyptic vision of the future. The new generation made the point that there is no planet B and that to ignore climate change will be fatal to civilisation as we know it. This initiative of Youth4Climate has inspired other organisations and people, including Elders' Climate Action or Extinction Rebellion, who demand more respect for and sustained contact with nature's regenerative power. They are all in favour of more openness and all are determined to oppose anyone who tries to appropriate what belongs to the planet, including those who continue to announce more appropriations of natural resources and superhighways to the stars and planets.

Although the introduction of green technologies has already brought noticeable changes with regard to sustainability, the most urgent topic to be addressed concerns the human impact on the future evolution of the planet. In fact, ecological matters should include the aforementioned perspective of an existential climate change. Awareness campaigns for natural resources, for the reduction of waste incineration can be regarded as the first hesitant steps before a philosophical ecology can be implemented, founded on choices with a beneficial impact on nature and on individuals who recognise its necessity. But the global management of the planet cannot be reduced to a set of norms and the rule of law, to conventions aimed at managing scarce natural resources, if all of this is not based on reflection and awareness at the time when even positive human energy is becoming scarce as it becomes absorbed by crisis management. The philosophical ecology we refer to here may produce its beneficial effects if it is based on the insight that whoever deliberately mistreats living beings, abuses life itself. Are we able to repeat after Zarathustra that "mother earth is our refuge" (46,8) and reformulate the idea of "remaining true to the earth" from Spitama's perspective?

Ecosophy

To include a contemporary approach on philosophical ecology in this book was an idea based on the finding that the chances of making the regenerative fire last are no worse today than they were before. I am referring here not to the numbers of people involved in a sustainable approach, but to the depth and intensity with which individuals become aware of the fact that "mother earth has been created to bring joy" (47,3). The Zoroastrian tradition is based on respect for the environment and for the production of adequate food[20]. It is a horticultural, agricultural and arboricultural tradition. To grow flowers and vegetables and to enjoy the company of animals actually provides a sense of prosperity within a community and has provided a haven of care and safety in contrast with the harsh life outside. The Zoroastrian brotherhood mentioned in the *Gathas* is an example of a community built on understanding and cooperation, motivated by the divine laws of nature. This has led to bounteousness, which in turn has engendered benefits for those who are in need. Hence, the importance attached in later Zoroastrianism to sharing, which shows that success and awareness of life's generosity can go hand in hand.

Every sunrise brings a new day and, for Zoroastrians, a new occasion to be thankful and express their openness to what the day holds in store for them. Every year, the new day is celebrated by Zoroastrians on a planetary level; *nov ruz,* new year, the beginning of spring. As we have seen, this rebirth of nature is essential and it has a highly symbolic character. The recognition of human life depending on nature's regeneration finds its expression in festivals that reflect the harmony of the components of life and in beautiful ritual practices like tree planting at birth and death or in the purification of water rituals that also include the protection of clean air. If

---

20   Once again, the protecting and healing quality of the elements of nature that provides prosperity and fertility should be emphasised. Everything that is life-giving is worthy of respect and should be protected, with reference to daily care and hygiene and in relation with mental consistency and what provides spiritual well-being.

we pursue this line of thought, to renew this arch-practice may be a way of happily combining our present-day lifestyles with ecological wisdom, with ecosophical choices.

The expression *ecosophy* was introduced by the French philosopher Felix Guattari, who also maintained that to engage in a good environment is not something that can be restricted to the protection of the planet only. As stated in *The Three Ecologies*, published in 1989, an environmental ecology should be integrally treated with a social ecology and with a mental ecology. Ecosophy between what is called the three ecological registers (environment, social relations and human subjectivity) may well provide an answer to the ecological crisis, Guattari maintains[21]. Only an ecosophical perspective on the conception of subjectivity will allow us to address the ecological perturbations of the environment, he argues. Answers can be found only "on a planetary scale and provided there is a political, social and cultural revolution that will reorient the objectives of the production of material and immaterial goods".

According to Guattari, issues like climate change should be addressed through an ethical-political ecosophy, because they are signals of a more deep-rooted ill. The necessary revolution will involve not only the visible power relationships, but also the molecular domains of sensitivity, intelligence and longing, since what goes wrong is related to the way life and social life is conducted on this planet. Guattari comes to the same conclusions as Zarathustra: to enjoy relationships with people who also care for nature's beauty is a way of building mutual strength. Solidarity in the world view that is put forward here implies that the beauty of all livings beings should be protected by individuals who are open to response-ability, which of course does not mean that these relations are free from conflict and misunderstandings, but that they can be consolidated when they do not only occur in an accusing frame of mind.

So, to implement response-ability in our life is about the readiness to make thought through choices in our relations with caring individuals[22]. We

---

21 Félix Guattari, *Les Trois Ecologies* (Paris, Galilée, 1989, p. 13 and 23 for the following quotation).

22 In today's world, we are fortunate to be able to share real friendships at a distance, which allow us to inspire each other, albeit sporadically. In my latest book in Dutch, I develop the topic of *voltaic friendship* – Alessandro Volta was the inventor of batteries – with the intention to distinguish between relationships that

are asked to take into account the vulnerability of all things and to reject the personal advantages stemming from treacherous or parasitic practices. Such advantages can easily turn into disadvantages that are not existentially fruitful. Again, it is not enough to find a revitalising way of life on our own, since it is crucial to develop courage and truthfulness, along with enthusiasm and the power of brotherly love (53,9) and to engage in relationships that can liberate an unforeseen strength, which in turn will stimulate inner growth (43,15). Zarathustra assumed that through self-examination, responsible choices and personal commitment, individuals could liberate inside themselves what is held in captivity and that is screaming to be let free. Could he have been right? Can we confirm that the immersion from childhood onwards in a process of liberation, in an ongoing process of renewing one's choices, is to learn how to face indecisiveness instead of adopting an indifferent attitude. Thus Zarathustra's reply: "He who listens to what is most true and carries it out during his life restores the wisdom inside of him" (31,19).

The present-day engagement with Zarathustra's thoughts requires us to keep translating them into our 'own' language. It makes us acknowledge an almost timeless concern typical of human existence. It is not so surprising that some individuals, even in very remote times, were aware of the mental frames that imprisoned them. In their confrontation with the oppression of their fellow-men, they denounced the hypocrisy of men of power and refused to bargain with them. For the sake of the community life, they encouraged each other to take their lives into their own hands and to follow the predetermined course of nature to reach completion. The cosmopolitans of tomorrow might acknowledge this and consider that the non-coercive freedom to become who we are can function as a symbolic tool. To say yes to life, in Nietzschean terms, is about perseverance, however heavy the burden we have to bear, provided we feel confident that we are not striving alone. Striving together to achieve a goal constitutes the horizon of our actions, even if results do not always live up to expectations. We wake each morning; our whole lifetime is an ongoing process of increasing awakening. It was Nietzsche who caught the spirit of revitalisation in this ancient oriental wisdom, though not its social dimension and the proto-ecology it also incorporates.

---

lose strength or wear out in the long run and durable relationships that allow us to regularly recharge our batteries.

Timeless reply

To reply literally means 'to fold back' (*replicare*), to bend back unto ourselves, trying to find a suitable response. In creating a space to reflect, we make it possible to transform an irresponsible reaction into a more responsible action. If the other party has been waiting for an immediate reaction, this might have turned out differently. It is essential that the two parties do not become entangled in a chain reaction and engage in a suitable response that requires responsiveness. In carefully considering the choices we make and responding to the best of our ability, responsibility appears not to be about feeling guilty and making up for mistakes. Response-ability focusses not just on the ability to choose right or wrong, but on enabling ourselves to make lasting choices. For the scream of mother earth to receive a response even today, our actions should be more in harmony with the self-regulative power of nature.

Zarathustra's proto-ecology addresses each concerned person on the basis of equality, and more specifically, on the basis of the equality of potential. Every single potential in humans is different and all humans have the capacity to progress towards completion and so participate in the overall process towards more wisdom (33,6). The word capacity refers to an inborn ability that needs to be learned to become a capability. The equality of potential to live a rewarding life means that human dignity cannot be restricted to those who claim the right to be respected, that dignity is revived in the fight against inaccuracies as a free choice. Of course, if the message can be heard everywhere, not all will lend a listening ear to it. Not everyone has yet met a good guide, which is why good leaders should continue to try and reach those "who are deeper in confusion" (49,1).

As Pico della Mirandola observed in his study on dignity, also called 'Manifest of Renaissance', humans can change themselves through their own free will. In his assertion that the exercise of intellectual capacities is essential in becoming dignified persons, Pico situated the root of dignity in the capacity to see the beauty of an ingenious order reflected in our surrounding; in the capability to learn from nature as a symbolic reflection of divine wisdom. Bearing this in mind, the idea of becoming a dignified person contains a parameter of determination. This is why I venture to posit that we are not in need of yet more revolutionary ideas. What is really needed is for us to gain self-confidence through strength-giving potentials; to gain more dignity through perseverance. No cosmopolitics, then, no cosmopolite politics beyond the boundaries of religions and nations is prospected in this book, but the renewal of a proto-philosophy, of an ecosophy, similar to that expressed in the *Gathas*, by individuals who succeed in becoming reliable persons and in responding to their potential.

The leaders of tomorrow should prepare to become steadfast individuals who understand or have experienced the destructive force of falsehood. When Isabelle Stengers underlines the fact that politics without a cosmos is irrelevant, she rightly urges for a politic discourse that does not say what ought to be, but one that is thought-provoking[23]. Rather than rely on the miracle of decisions that puts everyone into agreement, says Stengers, the personal initiative of rethinking one's life should be stimulated, preferably on a large scale. This idea can be traced back to the *Gathas*. In seeking for answers that may ensure the survival of the planet, we may consider that ecological decisions enforced top-down are one thing, but that another is the individual decision to confront powerlessness and gain more confidence in oneself.

Seen from a different angle to Nietzsche's ultimate disappointment in man, Zarathustra looked far ahead without anticipating. On the long run, humans cannot but put steps in the foreseen direction, inherent to nature's self-regulation. His vision of liberation was based on a slow and careful process of indirect action, which seemed to offer the most lasting prospect. By contrast, supporters of direct action will mostly depend on the overthrow of existing powers and their replacement by better leaders. They rely on a top down approach, which in the best of cases requires that a rule-giving instance be responsible for law and order. Indirect action is ruled from the bottom up and depends less on enforcement and control. Experience tells us that the voluntary engagement of co-workers who comply with directives they help to produce is more likely to achieve good results. It makes me wonder whether these verses can provide inspiration on a mazdaphilic basis, considering that a contemporary approach of this arch-practice requires not unconditional, but renewable trust. Otherwise stated: "All persons do their duty and become more confident in themselves" (53,4).

---

23 Isabelle Stengers, *Cosmopolitics I* (Minneapolis/London, University of Minnesota, 2010).

Indirect action

Probably because we recognise this problematic, we can imagine Zarathustra constantly on his guard, trying to find the right way to prevent his fellow-citizens from beginning to appreciate hypocrisy. "You who have kept away hatred and have resisted violence, hold on to good mind", he urged (48,7). As then, these words may resonate in the head and hearts of individuals who experience powerlessness, which in the long run causes distress and despair and makes them surrender. Sometimes resignation may even appear as a wise conclusion, especially if we are no longer able to distinguish between serene abandonment and defeatism. Zarathustra certainly experienced moments of despair, but he went on relying on the presence of individuals who resist what is silently killing them from the inside; individuals who refuse to give in to the enemy of life and understand the importance of inner communication with the eyes of the heart; who try not to copy mindless actions; who understand how they can deal with violent outbursts around them and who inspire each other in their love for life.

True empowerment of the people may come from scarcity and necessity, although it may also stem from a process of unmasking the self-interested leaders at the top, who try to convince others that misleading is the best way to safeguard one's own welfare. It may take decennia, even centuries, before false power is exposed and before conclusive action is taken. What is important is that individuals continue to examine their own view of the world and when the time comes that they seize the opportunity to make a difference. I am not referring here to unpredictable upheavals of indignation, but to current examples of ethical-ecological ways of life induced by individuals who feel it is not worthwhile to proceed with destructive or senseless activities.

For instance, the phenomenon called 'downshifting' is a defence of anti-consumerism and sustainability[24]. Downshifters try to address the unrestrained race towards success and curb social competition that threatens lasting friendship. The goal of downshifters is to discourage unwanted leisure

---

24 Downshifters seek to slow down and work fewer hours in order to have time for more important things in life. They value money and possessions less than health and peace of mind, which might indicate it is time for the transition towards less consumption and the possibly gradual reduction of our ecological footprint. Still popular today is Henry David Thoreau's description of the simple life he led in a self-built cabin in the forest (*Walden*, 1854).

activities caused by workaholism. In searching for a better balance between work and leisure, the emphasis is on building interesting relationships and on personal fulfilment. To enjoy the good things in life today is linked to scarcity and to the preservation of what is still available to us, which is why I perceive downshifting as a form of indirect action in expectation of more proof of the ecological urgency, both environmental and mental. Most encouraging is the downshifters' determination to build a trustworthy society. Examples of downshifters include Zarathustra, Buddha, Lao-Tse, Confucius and Gandhi, who did not indulge false power and led a sustainable way of life that was adopted by others. In others words, they were concerned with what is everlasting and with the human longing for this.

A timeless reply is perceivable, as Zarathustra stated, among those who are "eager to catch the notes the lovers of wisdom are singing" (50,4). This is why I trust the 'dead' language to give life to so many admirers of nature's beauty, also in the next millennium. Again, not the authenticity of the original message, but the renewal of the primordial choice, of 'our' renewal, of 'our' primordial choice is raised in the present book. I can honestly confirm that my becoming more familiar with Zarathustra's thinking has incited me not only to engage in this arch-practice and exchange views on it, but also to undertake a most personal small-scale action. Indeed, had I not felt personally challenged, I would not have arrived at this reply to destructive impulses: 'not me'. These two words are the expression of my personal silent response. What I have personally experienced as a necessary withdrawal from what is not life-giving, has made me discover indeed the valorisation of indirect action[25].

This withdrawal is not to be mistaken for a withdrawal from social, educational, political or economic life, nor should it be seen as a retreat into an ascetic or epicurean way of life, but as a reasonable choice on the basis of the arch-practice or proto-philosophy developed in this book. To withdraw from what tends to be destructive or seems to cause more destruction, appeared

---

25 This most personal commitment began in Isfahan (Iran) and it was shared with some friends in my hometown in Belgium, in 2017, on 1st May. This small-scale silent response not to give in to what cannot receive our consent (to say 'no') is necessarily linked to saying 'yes', to the constant reaffirmation of the tripartite motto. Friends who individually subscribe to this TACIT engagement are connected, not through a digital declaration of friendship, but in their factual confirmation of their commitment, day by day. TACIT stands for Till All Citizens Inspire Themselves, a movement forward, which is indeed utopian.

at a given moment to constitute a reasonable reply to destructive impulses. My repeated confrontation with the two tendencies inside allowed me to recognise these opposite tendencies also in others and in the outside world. It brought me to the primordial choice as I became more familiar with how to resist untrue, destructive tendencies, especially through a silently expressed 'not me'. Since then, this 'not me' reply is lived as a small contribution to life: I will not give my cooperation to what I have no reason to value. I will not give energy to what is causing damage by wilful deceit. At the same time, this silent recognition receives a welcome back-up from a regenerative element. The 'no' is based on the company of a 'yes'.

Indeed, the acknowledgment of the two tendencies and the tripartite motto can function as beacons or guidelines in this undertaking of saying no to non-life and yes to life. As I have experienced others to do the same, we no longer lend service to what is causing devastation, even if no one can prevent the urge to destroy that is inherent in all beings. When the expression 'not me' finds a shared space, it enhances the impression that one is not alone in the world coping with wrongful acts. To resist consistently and not violently to injustices, which by the way should not be confused with self-protection, is an inherent capacity of the human mind that many before us have revived and that can be unconditionally revalidated. What is needed is individuals who co-operate with the self-regulative dynamism of the universe, also at work in sound relationships. Just like gravity or quantum influence at a distance, such reviving is part of the ingenuity of nature, or of divine wisdom, and enables us to provide an appropriate reply. In two words, the 'not me' reply is a suggestion to invigorate the resistance to indifference or indolence and to activate perseverance. It expresses the timeless and silent determination not to give in to what cannot receive our consent.

Arch-practice

Because of the durable way of life implied in mazdaphilia, I wonder if younger generations could become more acquainted with this ancient knowledge; whether this arch-practice could be shared in social media, on platforms of discussion and in the sharing of mutual concerns. Without needing to moralise, school programmes could include the ancient wisdom of the *Vedas* and the *Gathas*, and propose a revitalisation of what humanity offered at the beginning of time as a daily practice. An inspiring form of sociability on a local level could eventually bloom on a broader level, thereby ensuring that young people are not cut off from basic values like honesty, confidence, perseverance in their private endeavours, and from the feeling that these are values that matter most.

What Zarathustra Spitama had in mind was not to produce strong individuals who would set an example that others could follow in support of the society of tomorrow, but the discovery of an energy that could be activated for the good of all. This empowering dimension resides in all living beings, not as an instinct similar to the survival of the fittest, but as a force that needs to be reinvigorated. Reinvigoration refers to active strength (Latin *vigor*), to the force of body or mind, and it holds a connotation of liveliness. It is derived from the Proto-Indo-European root *weg*, related to 'become awake', to enliven. To be alive is not a one-time gift, at birth, since life depends on a drive that is to be reactivated, rebooted, time and time again. In the Gathic conception, the person who chooses for a long-term relation with true thoughts, words and deeds, at a given time decides to confront inner contradictions and exercises in enhancing liveliness. It might take some time before this becomes a common practice, but it is surely worthwhile to discover this alternative to the passive state of living subsequent to what others consider valid.

To listen with an inner ear does not mean that we try to unveil the deep longings or discover the hidden superego (*Über-Ich*) in the Freudian's sense; a moral conscience which allows perversions to be sublimated. Neither do we comfort ourselves in the perdition of optimistic thoughts, of 'positive thinking'. It is rather a case of ascertaining our existential choices by gradually assigning value to what is true. We do not therefore free ourselves from certain conditions, but find in ourselves the conditions that liberate us from being who we are not.

In the 1980s, the interactive relationship with a changing reality found expression in the 'capability approach' of the Indian philosopher Amartya Sen[26]. Sen focused on the individuals' capability of achieving the way of

---

26 Sen won the Nobel Prize for Economy in 1998 for his contribution to the economy of welfare and well-being. He is an inheritor of the heterogeneous culture of India, with special attention devoted to Indian culture, history and identity and to issues such as inequality and poverty. To see India not like a Hindu country, but as a place where a range of religions coexist, is not the vindication of a secular project and should rather be regarded as the historical reaffirmation of the pluralist structure of the human mind.

life they have reason to value. He did not, almost in a transcendental vision, associate justice with a perfect and just society, because then, there is too much focus on putting institutions in order and too little attention is paid to actual injustices. Sen observed that people should be able to compare situations not by economic calculations, but by evaluating their personal chances and recognising opportunities. So there needs to be a shift from financial means, Sen argued, to actual possibilities, to capabilities.

This pragmatic approach centred on capabilities focuses on learning how personal talents can be developed and differs from Zarathustra's emphasis on potentials. We may indeed gradually discover our talents and find our place in the world, but a different perspective is to incite yourself to contribute to the nutrient cycle of life. Especially when this is lived as an active taking part in the process itself of progressively coming to completion. In the beginning, this may be perceived as the germination of a seed that has been planted in every single human being, but on the broader scale takes on the appearance of an active contribution to life's process, including for future generations. This kind of mental extension in time and space drives humans to finding out by themselves that reaching happiness may seem unrealistic, but that it is truly a meaningful direction they can give to their lives. Sooner or later, they discover the arch-practice of liberating themselves from the constructed character of the selves they have piled up over time.

Zarathustra's reply to the existential questions of current generations boils down to this: try to liberate yourself from injustices towards yourself and others, including animals and plants, and from what keeps you from becoming a nurturing rather than a devouring being. Zarathustra was aware of the benefits of a nourishing environment and acknowledged the happiness of whomsoever does not reduce friendship to the advantages friends can offer. He had a special insight into the human mind and did not invent new thoughts, but he inspired his interlocutors to examine their mutual conflicts and to consider taking non-violent actions. He sought friendship with individuals who share one another's insights on building a trustworthy society, with respect for other lifeforms on earth.

Mazdaphilia – unless the notion 'arch-practice' seems more appropriate – offers the prospect of responding to the challenges of the time. A person's viewpoint on life has a great deal to do with his or her approach of time, with the value he or she assigns to past events or future possibilities, with the way he or she conceives of the idea of starting anew, or with the chances that occur of seeing things with a fresh eye. There is the visualisation of an on-going movement from the beginning to a final point of arrival, from A to Z according to a linear or causal logic. And there is the conception of time similar to an arrow going from one place and back again, from Z to A, which can be perceived as a return to the beginning. Cyclic viewpoints are based on the emergence or regular recurrence of new starting points, possibly in a spiral movement. The openness to new chances, from Z to A, as reflected in the name of Zarathustra, implies that no end is final. This way, something that appears to be at risk of digressing may also be seen as an opportunity for a new start.

Re: Zarathustra

Let us reread the passage on the big event known as choice, when men and women, "whether they say true or false, whether they speak knowingly or not" they can "overcome their doubts by their dedication" (31,12). Zarathustra's reply to the challenges of his time sounds like a timeless invitation that makes us wonder to what extent it can appeal to us today. Can it still function as a sounding board in our singular existential process? And what is our reply to the everlasting return of opposite forces in combat that appears to be the self-replicating material of human life? Is it really the carrier of the casting material of daily reality? If it holds true that free choice is the human answer to the existential struggle and the tripartite motto the instrument for fine-tuning the singular existential instructions, then this arch-structure of life, with its arch-instructions, will speak to us over and over again; it tells us: this time, you cannot escape, you cannot hide.

This, in a nutshell, is how these age-old thoughts can transmit the arch-choice not to flee and to face existential struggles. To be confronted with reality, with what is real, is not the exception, but the true course of life. It implies a peculiar way of wading through existential abysses in our attempts to cope with what seems insurmountable. Since it is there, the nameless desire for completion, the progressive movement towards the accomplishment of a potential. The greatness of the 'eternal return' of the two opposite tendencies is that it can be picked up by humans who gaze at nature, at the sun, moon and stars and discover the beginning of an answer in the primordial choice; who retrace the periodic renewal of nature and the cosmic cycle of eternal return, which is so immense and brilliant that it enhances the longing for what is everlasting. Humans have an inborn necessity to remain in contact with regenerative energy, with what presents itself as an infinite energy. It makes them put themselves on the line and occasionally liberates the joyful return of an energy they feared was lost.

Freedom, Zarathustra knew, is not about the illusion of doing what you like, but about liberating yourself from what keeps you imprisoned in delusions. And so, he urged men and women, with determination, to guide themselves towards a truer self, to a point where they no longer allow themselves to cause harm in a thoughtless manner. He strived for progressing together until blooming, in agreement with what is given, and he kept repeating his dream "to fulfil the guardianship as planned" (33,6). He made men and women aware of the hidden working power they can address "in order to achieve the ultimate goal of a long life in harmony with trueness" (33,5). If they do not, and if they are interested in power (be it social, religious or political), he assumed they would have to learn how to resist it the hard way.

If more people feel surrounded by so many other people who refuse to give in to indifference, this can have a beneficial effect. If only inasmuch as the readiness to pay attention to injustice, great or small, is enhanced and the impact of malpractices is countered. It is up to the readers of these verses to ask themselves how far they can go in terms of contributing to a fairer sociability; to examine whether the regular practice of probing their motivations, deep down inside themselves, really is connected to a broader worldview, possibly even to cosmic dynamism. And to what extent they wish to improve their co-responsiveness, making them truly more involved in durable relationships and in accord with all that comes to life.

This is how Zarathustra expressed his dream of humanity and had he been able to spread his message over the internet, he would have made all earth dwellers aware of their unsuspected freedom. This at least was his understanding of the conscious involvement in a process towards accomplishment by individuals who constantly renew and revive the arch-choice. The importance of the true act is an appealing arch-practice directed towards the liberating potential of individuals who truly care about regenerative energy. Did Zarathustra assume the full development of humanity can each time better be identified, especially after bad choices have been made? This would explain that the whole venture was not just his personal quest, but the quest of humanity. When he urged his companions to give friendship and warmth to those who joined him in this quest, he gave a voice to the desire of humankind to become human and let them in on his idea "to construct a new and regenerated world" (46,13).

Had anyone asked Zarathustra whether good times were ahead, he would probably have replied: "Let each one choose" (53,2). We are free to choose a progressive, committed way of life, and we can also choose differently, or even not choose. Nevertheless, freedom of choice is not just based on the content of our choices, but on our commitment. For instance, in saying yes to the tripartite motto, we say yes to the act of choosing itself. It is a way of progressively discovering the meaning of the verse: "Action, not inaction, higher stands" (46,17).

MIMESIS GROUP
www.mimesis-group.com

MIMESIS INTERNATIONAL
www.mimesisinternational.com
info@mimesisinternational.com

MIMESIS EDIZIONI
www.mimesisedizioni.it
mimesis@mimesisedizioni.it

ÉDITIONS MIMÉSIS
www.editionsmimesis.fr
info@editionsmimesis.fr

MIMESIS COMMUNICATION
www.mim-c.net

MIMESIS EU
www.mim-eu.com

Printed by
Rotomail Italia S.p.A.
July 2025

www.ingramcontent.com/pod-product-compliance
Lightning Source LLC
Chambersburg PA
CBHW060835190426
43197CB00040B/2625